In the Circle of White Stones

STUDIES ON ETHNIC GROUPS IN CHINA

Stevan Harrell, Editor

IN THE CIRCLE
OF WHITE STONES

Moving through Seasons with
Nomads of Eastern Tibet

— * —

GILLIAN G. TAN

UNIVERSITY *of* WASHINGTON PRESS | SEATTLE *&* LONDON

In the Circle of White Stones was published with the assistance of a grant from the Naomi B. Pascal Editor's Endowment, supported through the generosity of Nancy Alvord, Dorothy and David Anthony, Janet and John Creighton, Patti Knowles, Katherine and Douglass Raff, Mary McLellan Williams, and other donors.

© 2017 by the University of Washington Press
Printed and bound in the United States of America
Composed in Minion Pro, a typeface designed by Robert Slimbach
20 19 18 17 16   5 4 3 2 1

UNIVERSITY OF WASHINGTON PRESS
www.washington.edu/uwpress

Library of Congress Cataloging-in-Publication Data
Names: Tan, Gillian G.
Title: In the circle of white stones : moving through seasons with nomads of eastern Tibet / Gillian G. Tan.
Description: Seattle : University of Washington Press, 2017. | Series: Studies on ethnic groups in China | Includes bibliographical references and index.
Identifiers: LCCN 2016011419 | ISBN 9780295999470 (hardcover : acid-free paper) | ISBN 9780295999487 (paperback : acid-free paper)
Subjects: LCSH: Tibet, Plateau of—Social life and customs. | Nomads—Tibet,Plateau of—Social life and customs. | Seasons—Tibet, Plateau of. |Pastoral systems—Tibet, Plateau of. | Buddhists—Tibet, Plateau of—Social life and customs. | Tibet, Plateau of—Religious life andcustoms. | Tan, Gillian G.—Travel—Tibet, Plateau of. | Tibet, Plateauof—Description and travel. | Ethnology—Tibet, Plateau of. | Tibet, Plateau of—Ethnic relations.
Classification: LCC DS786 .T33 2017 | DDC 305.9/0691809515—dc23
LC record available at https://lccn.loc.gov/2016011419

The paper used in this publication is acid-free and meets the minimum requirements of American National Standard for Information Sciences—Permanence of Paper for Printed Library Materials, ANSI Z39.48-1984. ∞

To my parents, Jit and Sheila, for their complete love.

Contents

Foreword

STEVAN HARRELL

There is a lot we can read about Tibet and Tibetans. There is no shortage of literature on its Buddhism, on its leaders, on its scenery and its environment, on its troubled relationship with various Chinese regimes over the years. But there is less that we can read on the lives of ordinary Tibetans, outside the storms of national and international politics, religious for sure but not necessarily particularly devout or knowledgeable. We read a lot about dissident lamas and articulate bloggers, about people who sacrifice themselves for their higher ideals. But we read a lot less about common people and how they pass their days and make their living in their stark and inhospitable environment, or about how the challenges of politics, policy, and globalization affect farmers and herders. Who are these people, with their proud and tragic history, who have attracted so much attention and often so little understanding from the rest of the world?

With *In the Circle of White Stones*, Gillian G. Tan begins to fill in some of the gaps in our knowledge, and she does it in the form of her own story. An ethnic Chinese, born in Malaysia, educated in the United States and Australia, she worked for several years for a US-based development organization operating in eastern Tibet. Unsatisfied with development as a career, she taught English for a while in a very provincial town but then turned toward academic research, focusing on the daily lives of the people in the same region where she had once been an aid worker and teacher.

In the Circle of White Stones is Tan's story of how she learned to know the people of Dora Karmo intimately by participating in their yearly round of making a living, by sharing the joys and sorrows of birth, marriage, and death, and by observing and sometimes participating in their interactions with a charismatic local lama who started a boarding school with the cooperation of local government authorities.

The people of Dora Karmo are what the Tibetans call *drogpa*, "those of the high pastures," in other words, nomadic pastoralists. At elevations ranging from a mere 3,900 meters at their wintertime stone houses up to 4,400 meters in their black tents in their highest summer pastures, they follow the animals who follow the sprouting, greening, and ripening of the grasses and then retreat in the winter when nothing grows and the snow descends. Tan takes us on a journey with one family—a widowed father, two daughters, and a son-in-law—as they complete this yearly round, gossip about their neighbors, fight and make up, and interact with Lama Dorje Tashi, who is at the same time a kinsman, a holy personage, a dedicated modernizer, and a skilled politician.

Life is hard—milking animals in the freezing rain, putting up heavy tents in storms, walking miles and miles over steep slopes at high altitudes—with nothing like electricity or running water or a soft bed. But family ties are close, stories are funny and fascinating, and Nyima Yangtso, as Tan was named by another important lama, finds true companionship and learns about more than just herding and milking as she follows the family through their migration, watches them grow through the addition of several grandchildren, and observes the community through years of wrenching but in many ways still hopeful social change.

In the Circle of White Stones thus shows us a different Tibet from what we read about in newspapers and on political blogs. Politics hovers in the background, as it must in any story of Tibet, and the inevitable but uncertain future of boarding schools and paved roads and Chinese language looms like the high-altitude weather—it will come and it will be stormy, but where, when, and how its force will be felt is impossible to know for now. We readers can only appreciate how Tan has documented what is probably a fading way of life and, in doing so, has preserved in print the humanity of the common people of Tibet.

Preface

The nomadic pastoralists of Minyag Dora Karmo are a community of around three hundred people who live in a high valley on the eastern fringe of the Tibetan plateau. At 3,900 meters, the valley itself is part of the Hengduan mountain system in Ganzi Tibetan Autonomous Prefecture, China. In the long, cold winter, Dora Karmo nomads stay in this valley, where they graze their yaks and live in simple stone-and-mud houses. In the spring, summer, and autumn months, the nomads live in black yak-hair tents so that they can move with their animals to a series of fresh pastures, going up to the highest altitude at the peak of summer. I lived with this community for a total of thirteen months in 2006, 2007, 2010, and 2013. This book is an account of my time in Dora Karmo.

It is often assumed that ethnographic fieldwork, during which a field-worker lives in intense interaction with the people of his or her field site, has a definite start and end. For me, however, the foundation for my fieldwork was in place before the period formally commenced in 2006. My experience in Tibetan areas of China began in 2000. I spent four years in Ganzi Prefecture, one of two Tibetan autonomous prefectures in Sichuan, before starting my academic research. During this time, I worked as an English-language teacher for a New York–based international development organization and then as a staff member at its field office in Chengdu, managing several projects in Dartsedo (Ch. Kangding)

County.[1] But more than that, I was in a domestic relationship with a Tibetan man from Dartsedo and, at that time, lived in a Tibetan world of familial and social relations. The people whom I came to regard as family members and friends greatly shaped and influenced my early years in the area.

This book presents two different views of Tibetan lifeways. The first is an immediate and intimate portrayal of everyday life in Dora Karmo, which includes descriptions of pastoral movements, details of daily chores and activities, interactions within a household and between neighboring households, conversations among family members and friends, and expressions of the personal feelings and thoughts of my various interlocutors. This portrayal, even though written in the "ethnographic present" (Hastrup 1990), is nevertheless based on my evolving relationship with Dora Karmo nomads over seven years. It is, therefore, closely connected with the second aim of this book: description of the unusual blend of strangeness and familiarity experienced during ethnographic fieldwork and reflections on the process of the ethnographic endeavor itself.

From a young age, I became habituated to the sense of being simultaneously a stranger and a familiar. I grew up in Malaysia as a fourth-generation Peranakan Chinese. I spoke English at home and went to the local Methodist church for Sunday school. At the same time, my family celebrated Chinese New Year and I attended government-run primary and secondary schools where the curriculum was delivered in Bahasa Malaysia. Many of my friends were Indian and Malay. Yet since childhood, I have felt simultaneously familiar and strange in the country of my birth. This combination of familiarity and estrangement enabled me not only to leave Malaysia without regret but also to feel at home in multiple places: I spent four undergraduate years in Santa Fe, New Mexico, a graduate year in Chicago, and almost seven years—coming and going—in New York City. What I describe may resonate with those who have had experiences like mine, as well as with those living in diaspora. The first

---

1 The 390 kilometers that separate Dartsedo and Chengdu, the capital of Sichuan, used to take two or three days to travel on a bus. This was in the old days, before the construction of both the Chengya highway from Chengdu to Ya'an and the Erlangshan tunnel through Erlang Mountain in the eastern Hengduan ranges. When I first traveled to Ganzi, the journey took just six and a half hours in a big four-wheel-drive vehicle owned by Kangding Vocational College. The tunnel had not yet opened to public transport, and I was lucky to be in a government car.

four years I lived in Ganzi Prefecture, I felt adept at handling its strangeness. The strangeness, moreover, was mitigated by my domestic familiarity with a trilingual and educated Tibetan man along with his friends and family members.

Before I went to live in Dora Karmo, my sense of self had already adapted to the Tibetan culture and way of life, yet I had never before lived with nomads, and on one earlier occasion, I had been physically and psychologically unable to persist at that high altitude. At this time and before I started my formal fieldwork, I had achieved only half of the necessary equation in a truly ethnographic endeavor: I was confident in my interactions with unfamiliar others, but I never truly risked my sense of self in the exposure (Jackson 2009). By the time I traveled to Dora Karmo, I was linguistically more competent, psychologically stronger, and physically fitter. Despite this, the challenges of constantly being with radically different others, of learning their specific inflection and vernacular of Kham Tibetan, and of earning the trust and respect of the people of Dora Karmo were more emotionally draining than what I had experienced. I also assumed, due to the depth and breadth of my experiences and friendships in the area, that the people of Dora Karmo would accept me without hesitation. I wanted, and expected, their approval. In all, fieldwork challenged what I thought I knew of Tibetan people, language, and culture.

The exotic in anthropology can be not merely that which is different or strange but that which challenges our understanding and, because of that, may be as much a property of the familiar and known (Kapferer 2013). After four years of English-language teaching, development work, and friendship, Tibetan people, language, and culture were not exotic for me, but, remarkably, by living with Dora Karmo nomads, they came to be in an anthropologically exotic relation with me, and I with them. We challenged our understandings of each other. Moreover, an intersubjective ethnography recognizes that inasmuch as ethnographers are discomfited by the threat to their sense of self, so, too, the people they live with are discomfited by their presence. The effort to communicate genuinely unsettles the certainties of those involved. I hope to convey something of this mutual process in the pages that follow.

This book is possible only because people in Ganzi Prefecture have given me their time and their friendship over the course of many years. While this has been a mutual and continuing exchange, I have always felt the odds were in my favor, that somehow I got more out of the exchange despite the unquantifiable nature of these gifts: the Tibetan name given to me by Zenkar Rinpoche, an incarnate lama closely linked to this particular area of Minyag; the gracious hospitality of the family I lived with in Dora Karmo; and the immeasurable advice and kindness of teachers at the provincial Tibetan school, to list but a few. The previous incarnation of Zenkar Rinpoche had spent many years meditating in the stone hermitages at the foot of Zhamo, the snowcapped, sacred mountain that looms over the high valley where Dora Karmo is located. Even before my arrival there, I sensed a deep connection to the place. Writing this book is my way of acknowledging these connections and expressing my gratitude.

Acknowledgments

Writing a book is a result of collaborations and conversations that do not always reveal themselves in the final product. These influences are far too numerous to recount, and I offer my deepest gratitude to those who have shaped, motivated, critiqued, and inspired me throughout my academic career.

I reiterate that this book has been possible only because of the friendships I have cultivated through many years of living, working, and researching in Ganzi Tibetan Autonomous Prefecture. I must single out special friendships with teachers and former students at the Sichuan Province Tibetan School and convey my sincere gratitude to Dorje Tashi, who with a twinkling eye and generous smile invited me to live at his golden stupa complex in Lhagang and then at his complex in Taraka for as long as I needed. For the people of Dora Karmo and especially for Gatsong household, my deepest appreciation for taking me in and putting me to work.

I would like to personally thank Stevan Harrell and Lorri Hagman for seeing that I had a story worth telling and supporting me through the unfamiliar process of academic book publishing. Special thanks to Sienna Craig, who generously engaged with a draft to give critical suggestions and sharpen my prose. I am grateful to Chandra Jayasuriya, who drew the maps in this book.

Finally, to Bob, who was my rock while this book went through several transformations.

Transcription,
Transliteration, and Names

I have used a roughly phonetic system of Tibetan transcription. The modifications have followed the pronunciation of Tibetan nomads of Dora Karmo (Kham dialect) and considerations of how a non-Tibetan-speaking reader might produce the words. A glossary of Tibetan and Chinese words at the end of the text lists the phonetic system of Tibetan transcription, the Wylie form of Tibetan transliteration, the words in Tibetan script, and the English translation. For transliterating Chinese, I have used the standard pinyin form. Terminology in the text is Tibetan unless distinguished as Chinese (Ch.).

An asterisk following the first occurrence of a name indicates that it is a pseudonym.

The People

*= pseudonym

IN DORA KARMO

Gatsong (2006–7)

Aku Kungo
Daka
Padka
Tsering Panjur

Gatsong (2013)

Aku Kungo
Daka
Kabzung Tsomo
Padka
Sonam Garjud
Tsering Panjur
Tsetruk Dorje
unnamed baby girl (Chumtso Kyid)

Rachor (2006–13)

Chonyi Wangmo
Gyurmed Gonbo
Pelma Lhaka
Pelma Tso
Wonam Drolma

Jonla (2006–13)

Aku Kunchok
Ani Tseko
Aku Palzang
Dhundrup Lhamo
Ratso
Sonam Tsanyi
Tebu
Tenzin Choga
Tsoko
Woje Tashi

Others in Dora Karmo

Ani Moko
Ani Palmo

IN LHAGANG TOWN

Aku Dorje*
Ala Lhamo*
Ala Soko
Tashi*

RELIGIOUS PERSONAE IN LHAGANG AND DERGE

Dorje Tashi (Aku Dordra), Jalse Rinpoche
Pelma Kabzung, Derge Dzogchen Rinpoche
Thubten Nyima, Zenkar Rinpoche

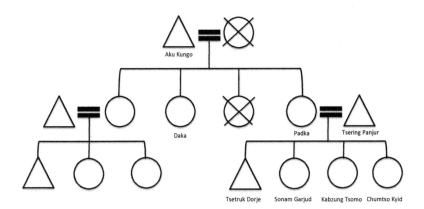

CHART 1
Kinship chart of Gatsong household.

Key
○ Female
△ Male
⊗ Deceased

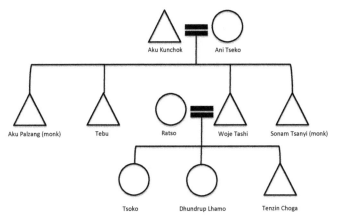

CHART 2
Kinship chart of Rachor household.

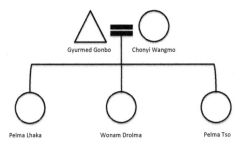

CHART 3
Kinship chart of Jonla household.

Timeline

National events (italic)
Author's activities in Tibetan regions (roman)

2000   *Chinese government announces the Develop the West cam-*
        paign; Ganzi Tibetan Autonomous Prefecture in Sichuan opens
        to foreigners

        Works as English teacher in Ganzi Prefecture

2001   Works in Sichuan field office of US nongovernmental
        organization

2003   Teaches English language and studies Tibetan language in
        Dartsedo, prefectural seat of Ganzi Prefecture; resides in
        Dartsedo town

        SARS outbreak in Hong Kong and China

2006–7 Conducts ethnographic fieldwork in Dora Karmo

2008   *Protests in Tibet*

2008   *Summer Olympics in Beijing*

2009   *First self-immolations on the Tibetan Plateau (Ngawa Prefecture, Sichuan)*

2009   *Regional governments crack down on foreign presence and activities in Tibetan areas of China*

2010   *Yushul earthquake in Yushul Prefecture, Qinghai*

        Conducts ethnographic fieldwork in Dora Karmo

2010–12   *Self-immolation protests intensify; surveillance of movements of people, Tibetans included, between regions of Tibetan Plateau, increases*

2013   Conducts ethnographic fieldwork in Dora Karmo

In the Circle of White Stones

CHAPTER 1

Getting to Dora Karmo

I arrived in Dora Karmo in the early morning light in the back of a small tin-can car that shook and rattled on the bumpy dirt road. The late winter cold had caused the grasslands to turn brown. This color contrasted sharply with the jagged rocky edges of Zhara mountain and the stark blue sky. The familiar sight of the mountain eased my nervous anticipation of what lay ahead. Would I be physically able in that environment? Would I be psychologically strong enough to withstand this fieldwork? The realization that Lhagang (Ch. Tagong) town, where I was coming from, was less than twenty-five kilometers away provided some reassurance. Lhagang was a place I had been arriving at, and leaving from, for the past five years. I had good friends there.

Lhagang in 2006 was still a "Wild West" sort of town, even though it was the administrative and social hub for eighteen administrative villages of nomadic pastoralists in the surrounding grasslands. Lhagang was also an administrative township in a county called Kangding, the prefectural seat of Ganzi, which was created in 1955 as an administrative Tibetan prefecture under the Chinese Communist Party. During the earlier Republican period (1911–49), the area of Ganzi was coterminous with eastern Xikang, and formed part of the historical Tibetan region of Kham (also known as Chubzhi Gangdrug, or Four Rivers, Six Ranges). Ganzi covers an area roughly the size of Nepal (150,000 sq km) and the almost one million people who live here are mostly Khampa Tibetans, known for being the most warrior-like of all Tibetans. Male Khampa nomads still strutted down Lhagang's single dusty street with long knives attached to their left hips and right thumbs hooked to the belts holding up their heavy *chubas*, or long Tibetan robes. A traveler would need to pass through Lhagang if using the northern branch of the Sichuan–Tibet highway, a winding and adventuresome road that looped almost four thousand kilometers between Chengdu and Lhasa.

Lhagang is home to a large Tibetan Buddhist monastery of the Sakya sect. The monastery sits cradled in a crescent created by three small hills: Chenrezig in the middle, Jambayang to the left, and Chana Dorje to the right. For local people, the hills are emanations of three major religious figures in Tibetan Buddhism: Phagpa Chenrezig (Avalokhiteshvara) representing Compassion, Jambayang (Manjushri) representing Wisdom, and Chana Dorje (Vajrapani) representing Power. In addition to its contemporary political, economic, and social significance for its townspeople, Lhagang holds particular religious, historical, and cultural significance for this region of the Tibetan plateau. The topography connects it deeply to narratives of Tibetan sacred geography, and the Jowo religious statue in its monastery links it strongly to the religious center of Lhasa, 1,700 kilometers west.

Lhagang was significant for me in several ways. The head lama of its Sakya monastery is Zenkar Rinpoche, who now lives in New York and gave me my Tibetan name in 2000 while I was working for Trace Foundation, a New York–based organization that had supported his study at Columbia University. Working with this foundation also introduced me to Dorje Tashi, the influential local incarnate lama from Dora Karmo who had established several key schools and cultural institutions in the Lhagang area. My evolving relationship with Dorje Tashi, who was first an acquaintance, then my student in English-language learning, then adviser on my research, and, finally, a friend, is detailed in chapter 5.

I traveled here frequently while I was an English-language teacher at the Kangding Vocational College in Gudrah town, about thirty-seven kilometers south of Dartsedo. When I arrived to teach English in 2000, Gudrah was a dusty one-street town with a handful of noodle restaurants and small shops selling sundry items. In my year there, the town's streetscape was transformed from old wooden houses to concrete buildings that were already dirty and gray from the process of construction. The

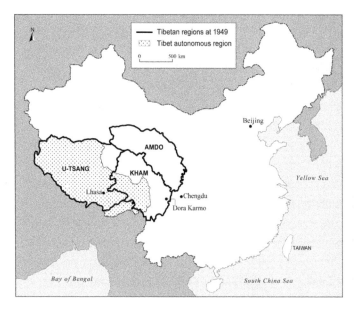

MAP 1
Tibet Autonomous
Region (shaded) overlaid
with estimated boundar-
ies of Tibetan regions
in 1949. Cartographer:
Chandra Jayasuriya

MAP 2
Sichuan, with detail
of Ganzi Tibetan
Autonomous Prefec-
ture. Cartographer:
Chandra Jayasuriya

vocational college had just built a new guesthouse, and the government had just finished constructing the Erlangshan tunnel. I was not aware of this at the time, but the flurry of construction was supported by the inflow of money to Sichuan as a result of the Develop the West (Ch. Xibu Dakaifa) campaign. As I was the first resident foreigner in the prefecture, the administrators and teachers at the vocational college, all Han, who were solely responsible for me, were acutely worried about me. In those initial months, as soon as I stepped out of my room in the guesthouse, an administrator or teacher would appear to take me to meals, classes, and trips to town. These appearances were usually accompanied by the remark "We are worried about your safety." When the administrators and teachers eventually tired of the responsibility, students took over. This constant tracking was immensely tedious and greatly influenced my first impressions of rural China. Lhagang was a place that I had gone to regularly in order to escape from the claustrophobic valley of Gudrah town.

In those early years, I made good friends in Lhagang, one of whom was a student at the Kangding Vocational College when I taught there. This friend, Tashi*, had studied English with me and diligently applied himself. He eventually enrolled in a well-regarded English-language training program for Tibetans. After receiving this training, he would return to Dartsedo County to teach English to Tibetan students at a local middle school, which in the Chinese educational system incorporated grades six through nine.

In 2006, I was staying in Tashi's family home in Lhagang and trying to think about the best way of organizing my stay in Dora Karmo. The person who would eventually help organize my stay in Dora Karmo was Tashi's cousin, a young man who had studied English in India and recently returned to Lhagang. He walked into the large, elaborately painted and decorated room where family members drank tea, ate meals, and watched television. Guests such as myself were hosted in this room. He looked at me, faintly surprised at finding an unexpected person in the room, before turning to his maternal aunt, Tashi's mother.

"She is Tashi's teacher," Ala Lhamo* said in her quiet manner. Then, slightly under her breath, she added, "She is a foreigner."

He turned to look at me and said, "Hello," in English.

"Hello," I replied in English. And then switching to Tibetan, I explained, "My name is Nyima Yangtso. I'm from Australia—well, I come from Malaysia, but I live in Australia now."

"Oh, do you speak Tibetan?" he asked, with surprise again in his eyes.

"Yes, a little," I replied. "I learned with teachers at the Sichuan Province Tibetan School." The school, located in Dartsedo town, is a middle-level vocational school (Ch. *zhongzhuan*) incorporating grades nine through twelve, and was distinctive because it provided a traditional Tibetan curriculum to local young Tibetans. This curriculum, taught in Tibetan language, included Tibetan medicine, Tibetan Buddhist philosophy, astrology, and painting *thangka* (traditional Tibetan cloth painting). The school had begun in 1981 in a tent in Dzogchen town. Significantly for me, Zenkar Rinpoche had played a key role in establishing the school and securing its present location in former army barracks outside Dartsedo.

"Oh, you speak our dialect well," Tashi's cousin remarked.

After some further small talk, it emerged that he had been a primary-school teacher in Dora Karmo for two years after his return from India. I was immediately attentive because this was an opportunity to enter Dora Karmo that was not associated with either Dorje Tashi or the development organization working in the area. Earlier that day, I had met a local acquaintance who knew some nomads from Dora Karmo. But she had been incredulous that I wanted to live with the nomads and mixed her assurances that she would help me with liberal doses of worry and doubt: life is very hard, there are no vegetables, they are dirty, it is cold, you are by yourself . . . the list went on. I doubted she would try her best. Meeting Tashi's cousin, then, signified a favorable alignment of the stars.

"Do you know a family in Dora Karmo that I can stay with for a few months?"

He looked at me and asked, "Why?"

I replied, "To learn more about Tibetan nomad culture and to learn nomad dialect. You see, I speak like a farmer because all my teachers are farmers!"

He laughed, and I continued, "I am a student now at my university in Australia. I want to learn about the nomad way of life. I want to live with a family and eat what they eat, work with them. I also want to understand what they think about the changes happening here." I gestured around me to indicate the larger Lhagang area. "For example, what do they think about this American development organization and its work?"

He listened to me carefully. While I was talking, the telephone rang. After I stopped talking, Ala Lhamo called to him and said, "Tashi wants to speak with you." Tashi had called at an opportune time. Through his cousin's replies, I gathered that my friend was instructing him to help me as best he could. When our conversation resumed, my conclusions were confirmed.

He said, "You can stay with the village teacher, I think. He is an older man with two daughters, maybe the same age as you. I will arrange it for you, don't worry." He paused and then added, "He is a good man."

I was grateful to him for helping me. The next day in Lhagang, I prepared for my initial stay of ten days in Dora Karmo, which would allow me to assess the situation for a much longer stay of six months. Even as I became familiar again with the town, I noted more changes in both the streetscape and the lifestyle. It made me recall past conversations in Dartsedo with teachers from the Sichuan Province Tibetan School who were also my teachers both in the Kham dialect of Tibetan language and in contemporary issues of Tibetan culture and society. From them, I learned innumerable facts about the present situation of Tibetans living in Ganzi, but I also learned about their childhoods in nomadic and farming areas of Kham in the late 1960s and early 1970s, about the Sichuan Province Tibetan School in its early years, first in Dzogchen town and then in Ta'u town, and about their concerns regarding the gradual erosion of Tibetan language and traditional Tibetan culture in Ganzi.

One conversation at one of my many lunches with these teachers, usually at a nearby Han restaurant, stood out.

"The problem now is that the culture holders are not the decision makers," said Teacher Palzang*.

He continued, "Of course culture is never permanent and fixed. Tibetan culture has been influenced by external forces for most of its history. But we have always had the choice to accept the beneficial things and to reject unnecessary aspects. Now change is happening so quickly that our culture is approached from all sides. The people who are making change are not the culture holders. And I think the most important thing we can do is to allow people to think and choose among the new things that are coming into Tibetan society."

Teacher Dorje* had been listening intently and nodded his head in agreement. "Ya ya, but how do they think and choose? That is also important. Before, maybe they didn't have to think and choose so much because there were not so many new things. But now, they have to choose all the time, yet they are not strong enough in their own ways, their own language, and their own culture. For example, *thangka* paintings. We have teachers here who are very good *thangka* painters. They were trained in the traditional way, and they have a good foundation in traditional methods. Now, if they were to change some small part of their paintings, to develop a new modern style of *thangka*, then I think it is OK. They have good knowledge about the traditional way. But now, more and more, we see *thangka* painters who do not have good knowledge but who paint modern *thangka*. Is their work good? I don't think so!"

"Eh, Yangtso, what he means is that everyone must come to our school to learn *thangka* painting!" Teacher Nyima* jokingly added.

"Yes, Teachers Sonam* and Tsering* [who teach *thangka* painting] will be very rich then!" Teacher Dorje laughingly added. There was laughter around the table as the conversation continued.

"This is a problem," said Teacher Palzang. "We think about it every year, because every year, the level of Tibetan language for our students is worse and worse. There will be a day when all we do is teach *ka kha ga nga*," he added ruefully, referring to the first four letters of the Tibetan alphabet.

Then in a matter-of-fact way, he added, "This school was started by great Tibetan scholars, such as Thubten Nyima [Zenkar Rinpoche]. It has produced great Tibetan scholars, like Tashi Tsering. Our students used to be taught by illustrious Tibetan scholars, including the Panchen Lama. And soon, it will teach *ka kha ga nga*."

Teacher Dorje said, "The problem is also with society, and we ourselves, as teachers, must be very careful. More and more I think that the teachers here are less committed. They are part of the changes that are happening in society. Look at Dartsedo and also farther out in Rangaka and Lhagang. With all the new buildings and tea shops, it is hard for us to focus on teaching let alone for the students to focus on learning. There are so many distractions now. And when the level of students becomes lower and lower, it is harder to be a committed teacher."

"You know, Yangtso," Teacher Nyima said to me, "I have started to use some of the teaching techniques that you used when you taught me English. I think some of those techniques are really useful; they helped me a lot!"

"Oh, thank you so much! I am so happy to know this," I said, delighted by this compliment.

I had followed their conversation in Tibetan with interest and only a little difficulty. Collectively, these were my Tibetan-language teachers. They were careful to use words that they knew I could understand, and they spoke clearly and slowly so that I would comprehend what they were saying. Nonetheless, my language skills at this time were developing quickly because, even though I had stopped working with Trace Foundation, I remained in Dartsedo for close to a year informally teaching at the school and informally learning Tibetan. It was mainly during this time, between 2003 and 2005, that I settled into a Tibetan way of life and began to feel very familiar with the mannerisms and habits of urban and intellectual Tibetans. I developed a sensibility toward Tibetan culture that, nevertheless, would be challenged when I started my formal fieldwork in Dora Karmo.

— * —

Two days after meeting Tashi's cousin, I was on my way to Dora Karmo. The bumpy journey was longer than expected. The grasslands swept out the nearer we came to the mountain range of Zhara, which loomed in impressive proximity the higher the little car chugged along. We sat in silence through most of the forty-minute ride until we arrived at the top of the pass and I took in my first view of Dora Karmo. Tashi's cousin turned back to smile at me.

"Your home," he said in Tibetan.

And what a remarkable home it was. Taraka was the first area I came to in Dora Karmo. Embraced by the foothills of Zhamo mountain, it marked the end of the dirt road and the beginning of a wide expanse of grassland valleys sweeping out to a panoramic vista accentuated by Minyag Gungkar, a majestic peak of 7,556 meters. The land was still brown and barren from winter, but the air was clear and crisp. As the little car made its way down, winding back and forth along switchbacks, Tashi's cousin gave a shout, and we stopped. He had spotted a *lawa*, or Tibetan musk deer, grazing on some shrubs on the hillside about one hundred meters from us. We hurried to grab my camera, and the animal graced us with one photo before it bounded out of sight. I took this as an auspicious omen, a good start to my fieldwork in the area.

But even then, I noticed the recent scarring of the landscape by the road that bore us to Dora Karmo. It divided Taraka in half, and from our vantage point, the landscape looked like someone had taken a blunt razor and cut across the plain. We descended past Azoma, a small hillock covered with prayer flags, and stopped where the road ended, abruptly, past a low wall of prayer stones in front of a stone house. The car pulled right, away from the house and the road, onto the grass. Some children were playing outside; they laughed and ran up to us as we got out of the car. I kept my telltale backpack out of sight for the time being. The children, about ten girls, were immediately shy, but then they recognized their former teacher and approached him, laughing. They stared brazenly at me, perhaps because I was wearing a long Tibetan robe but not in a style to which they were accustomed and because I looked *slightly* different: not obviously foreign, not really Han, and not Tibetan. This theme of *slightly* different would recur in my interactions with Dora Karmo nomads. Incidentally, because I was a foreigner, I also did not easily fit a common (and derogatory) Tibetan phrase: *ra ma lug*, which literally means "not goat, not sheep." This phrase is a variation of another phrase, *ja ma bod*, which means "not Chinese, not Tibetan" and is used to refer to people of mixed Han-Tibetan parentage.

Tashi's cousin and I approached a cluster of three buildings. The middle building was the largest and most imposing, a solid two-story configuration of earth and stone, punctuated with the slender slits of Tibetan windows of the style found in this nomadic community. This was the cooperative building that had been built more than twenty-five years ago under the collectivization policies of the Chinese state. To our right was a slightly dilapidated one-story building of the same style, which was the school. It had been built ten years ago with government money at around the same time the winter structures had been built for the nomads as part of the government's efforts to partially settle them. And to our left was a modest shed. Inside was a large prayer wheel, about one and a half meters in diameter, rotating around a three-meter-high wooden pole. Old people, especially, circumambulated the wheel while spinning it from a waist-high ledge and chanting prayers. A few old people emerged from the prayer wheel room, curious, as we made our way to the school to find the elderly teacher.

He was sitting in the school courtyard, sheltered by a trapezoid of shade created by the angle of the blazing sun on the eaves. The ground was dry and hard, another sign of winter's end. He looked at us when we entered the courtyard and greeted my contact with a calm smile. Our arrival had caused a slight stir in the morning quiet, but the atmosphere was peaceful all the same. He gestured for us to enter the dark room opposite the kitchen, the teacher's quarters.

"Ya, will you drink tea?" he asked, limping toward a makeshift stove fueled by dried yak dung.

"No, no, please sit, teacher," Tashi's cousin replied respectfully. I noticed that his manner had changed, and he had gone from a self-assured young man who had spent time living abroad to a quieter person.

He continued in a low tone, "She is Tashi's teacher, taught him English in Gudrah. She is a foreigner, a student. She would like to learn about a nomad's way of life and about Tibetan culture by living in Dora Karmo, eating, sleeping, and working here. Can she live in your house for six months? If she needs to travel to Lhagang, she can find her way on the road or maybe with one of your horses. Is that all right?"

The teacher listened with his head bent down. He asked, "Does she speak Tibetan?"

At this point, I chimed in, "I can speak Tibetan but not very well. And I don't really know nomad dialect."

The teacher looked at Tashi's cousin. He said something that I didn't fully catch and then concluded, "That is all right. She can go home with me after class."

I was surprised by the brevity of the conversation and the ease of the negotiations. It seemed that there should be more to discuss.

I asked Tashi's cousin, in English, "Should I offer to give money for my stay?"

Tashi's cousin replied in English, "OK, I will ask. Maybe you should go outside for a while."

I went outside to the sunny courtyard and wandered down a slope toward some yaks grazing the pastures. It was serene; the children had gone into the classroom, and the old people had retreated to the prayer wheel room.

When I returned, Tashi's cousin and the teacher were talking quietly.

Tashi's cousin said in English, "He doesn't want any money. And it's all right. You can stay with him and his daughters for six months. If you need to go to Lhagang, you can use their horses but maybe give them some money for that. Fifty *yuan* should be OK."

In less than twenty minutes, everything was arranged. Tashi's cousin drove away, and I waited for the teacher to finish his morning's classes before returning home with him.

Carrying my fifteen-kilogram backpack at an altitude of close to four thousand meters over the approximately two kilometers between the school and the teacher's winter house was hard work. Four girls of varying ages walked with us. In my attempt to lighten my load, I offered them each an apple from the large bag I had bought in Lhagang. The teacher declined and spoke little with me along the way. The girls, in contrast, and following our brief play together in the school courtyard, were full of curiosity and questions. They looked at my hands and measured theirs against mine.

They asked me questions, some of which I did not immediately understand, and then realizing that they could understand me well enough but it did not always work the other way around, they spoke more slowly. We introduced ourselves: Tsoko, eleven years old, born in the year of the Rat; Tashi Tsomo, eleven, also the year of the Rat; Kabzung Lhamo, twelve years old, the year of the Pig; Pelma Tso, nine years old, the year of the Ox; and myself, Nyima Yangtso (my Tibetan name), from Australia, born in the year of the Tiger. The teacher was called Aku Kungo. He walked with a limp in his right leg and was dressed in a traditional Tibetan *chuba* with a fox-fur-lined hat on his head. When we stopped so that I could rest and catch my breath, the girls took turns sitting beside him and hugging him; he was obviously beloved. As we walked around a bend in the path, the first girl, Tsoko, veered left to go to her own home. Within a hundred meters, Aku Kungo also veered left, and we said good-bye to the remaining three girls, who continued uphill to the right. The house in front of us was a small, single-story stone-and-mud building, set within a stone wall. Two ferocious Tibetan mastiffs were tied up in front of the entrance to the enclosure, and I tightly gripped the few stones I had picked up the moment I had seen them.

"Don't worry," Aku Kungo said, keeping himself between the dogs and me as we entered the enclosure.

A young Tibetan woman with an open, generous face and twinkling eyes walked out of the house. She was dressed in a dark purple-brown Tibetan *chuba*, and her hair was braided with red wool and wrapped around her head in the style of this area. She had a gold front tooth and a bright pink, fitted scarf around her neck.

"Are you tired?" she asked, looking at me.

"No," I replied, even though my lungs felt like they were going to explode.

I lowered my head to avoid hitting the top of the door frame and followed them into a dark space, through another low door frame to the left, a few paces down through another low door frame to the left, and into a room brightened by two small windows. Another Tibetan woman, similarly dressed, was in the room, and, after glancing quickly at me, she looked at Aku Kungo.

"Hello," I began, "my name is Nyima Yangtso."

The younger sister smiled at me, faint laughter in her eyes.

"What is your name?" I asked her.

"Padka," she replied.

I then turned to her older sister, who was still unsmiling, and asked, "What is your name?" I smiled broadly at her, hoping to convey friendship and my good intentions.

With an inscrutable stare out of a face framed by strong high cheekbones, she replied, "Daka."

"Oh," I said. I repeated my Tibetan name and then added, trying to make some sort of conversation, "Thank you for letting me stay." She turned away, toward Aku Kungo, who had told them to arrange my bed as he sat down on his and started turning his prayer wheel. There was a burst of activity. I stood helplessly aside as the two women moved altar bowls and items, sacks and bedding, low stools and pots, to make way for me and my large backpack. As they stood discussing which bedding to use, I volunteered that I had my own. At this point, I also gave them the bag of apples and other sundry items that I had acquired in Lhagang, hoping that this offering of gifts would make them feel more kindly toward me despite the disruption I was causing. Padka shyly took an apple and put it inside her Tibetan robe.

The name of the household was Gatsong.

CHAPTER 2

The House and the Tent

I awoke to the low hum of prayer chants. The dried twigs on the ceiling of the winter house slowly came into focus, and the worn leather bags of *tsampa*, the local staple of roasted barley flour, piled high to my left reminded me where I was. The room was cold. In his bed across from mine, Aku Kungo sat cross-legged with heavy blankets around him. His gray head was bent down as he chanted from a traditional Tibetan book, a long rectangle of loose-leaf pages kept between two wooden blocks. His daughters, Daka and Padka, had already woken to milk their female yaks, also known as *dri*.

Due to Aku Kungo's small salary as the village schoolteacher, their household situation was comfortable. The altar articles, hearth, pots, sundry items, and general tidiness of the room reflected this. The house itself consisted of two rooms. The space encountered immediately upon entering was the storeroom for dried yak dung, the principal source of fuel in nomadic areas, and doubled as the place where baby yaks were tied up for the night. Turning left into a narrow dark passage, and then left again almost immediately, one entered the inner living space, which measured less than thirty square meters. In this room, the family cooked, ate, slept, and prayed. This living space mirrored the general arrangement of the household's black yak-hair summer tent: the women's, or home, side was to the left of the entrance, and the men's, or guest, side was to the right. This room had no inner walls; one went out to the grasslands for privacy.

My first night with the household had been tentative, exploratory, polite. After my embarrassment at having displaced Daka from her bed, I was keen to be as helpful as possible. The sisters, Daka and Padka, keen to be as hospitable as possible, refused my offers of help and seated me on a folded felt square on the floor by the hearth. When Daka and Padka came back in the evening after having herded and tied up the animals for the night, Daka quickly lit the hearth using dried branches of a local potentilla shrub, called *fema*, and dried yak dung. She asked her father what she should make for dinner, glancing at me. He said to make rice and potatoes and to fry some green chilies, if they had any, with the potatoes. After filling a blackened kettle with what was left of the day's water, she left the room to fill the wooden bucket with more water. This was collected from a small puddle-size pool outside the front enclosure of the house using a long-handled metal ladle. I told Aku Kungo that I had brought my own *tsampa* flour, which I was happy to have for dinner. He smiled and told me to keep that. We would eat rice. The meal was extremely tasty. They had carefully cleaned all utensils and had given me my own plate of potatoes.

All the time up to the evening meal, I observed their movements and actions with curiosity and attention. Yet when we were ready to retire, the situation was reversed. When I reached for my large backpack, I became the focus of attention. As more and more things emerged from my backpack—headlamp, sleeping bag, notebook and pen, toothbrush, earplugs—they became more curious. Aku Kungo was particularly interested in the headlamp and asked if it used batteries. Daka and Padka shook their heads and stuck out their tongues when I pulled out my ever-expanding sleeping bag from its compact travel pouch. The extreme interest they showed in my things and actions was equal to the way in which I had become absorbed in their things and way of life.

The next day, there was a lingering smell of smoke from the yak dung fire as the early morning light entered through narrow, white plastic, sliding windows. Outside the windows, one looked directly south and across rows of unfolding mountaintops. On most days, the unmistakable outline of Minyag Gungkar towered in the distance. The only other house visible from this outlook belonged to the household called Jonla, the house of the village leader, Aku Kunchok. Despite their proximity, the households were not kin-related. Otherwise, the landscape was open and bare, apart from the black shapes of yaks grazing on mountain slopes. A wall of stone, topped with patties of dried yak dung, enclosed the area in front of the house. Beside the gate, one Tibetan mastiff tied to a pole by a heavy metal chain guarded the household. Although young, it was a ferocious creature with red eyes. The family rarely called it by its name and never let it off its chain in the winter pasture. The other, older dog mostly wandered, although it was still very much a guard dog. It had to be held during my first month living with the household until it became accustomed to me.

That first morning, we ate breakfast at half past seven after Daka and Padka finished milking the animals. Because it was still winter, the milk was scant and barely sufficient for the day's supply of milk tea. Nomads in this area drink only milk tea, saying that butter tea is for farmers farther down the valley. They watched intently while I reached into my small cloth bag filled with *tsampa* flour and kneaded it with milk tea and a spoonful of melting butter into a knobbly lump the size of a tennis ball. I commented self-consciously that I made *tsampa* like a farmer, poking my middle finger into the bowl to mix the ingredients before running my hand along the inside in circular motions to knead the ball. They, like other nomads I knew, were more graceful, deftly combining the ingredients by slowly running their hands along the rim of the bowl and then, as the ingredients became more combined, inside the bowl in circular motions that yielded the same result. Daka asked me where I had gotten my wooden bowl. I replied that it was a gift from a friend and teacher at the provincial Tibetan school who came from Derong, a farming county in the southernmost part of Ganzi Prefecture.

"He is a *rinpoche* from Derong," I added, eager to convey to them something of myself that I thought they would approve of. I did this because I was already slightly unnerved by how little I understood of their conversations with each other, how they carefully watched my every move, and how they both constantly looked at my hands. My hands were without adornment, simple hands, I thought, but, as I would eventually come to learn, Daka and Padka were fascinated by the skinniness of my hands, the small bones, my fair skin, and my (relatively) clean nails—telling indicators of how little I had labored in my life.

In contrast, they labored all day, every day. In the heart of winter, when fodder was not plentiful, they spent no more than an hour milking the *dri.* Then they had to lead the animals out to pasture, collect and dry yak dung for fuel, cook meals, carry water, collect kindling, and spin yarn from bundles of yak hair that they had meticulously pulled apart, loosening strands and removing dirt. As nomad women, all work related to children, *dri*, and the hearth fell to them. In addition, nomads in this area explained a further gendering of labor in the following way. Any work that required strength in the arms and shoulders—for example, cutting hair from animals and weaving yarn into cloth for the black tent—was done by men. Any work that required strength in the lower back and hips, such as collecting and carrying water and kindling, was done by women. These tasks were also closely associated with the main female responsibility of the hearth. A person, irrespective of age or gender, had a place in any household. Over the next six months, I was determined to find mine.

The household had four people. Aku Kungo's wife, from neighboring Shamalang, had passed away twenty-five years ago, and he had raised his daughters single-handedly. His oldest daughter had married a Tibetan government worker, and they lived more than two hundred kilometers away, in Lithang. They had three children, and the oldest, a boy, was studying in the local monastery of Dora Karmo. Daka was the second-born, and the same age as I. Padka was four years younger than Daka and eventually would call me "Achi Nyima," *achi* being the kinship term for "older sister." Padka's fiancé, Tsering Panjur, was the household's *magpa*, or called-in son-in-law, whose family lived in Shamalang. His mother, Bamu, had been born there, but his father, Thubten, came from a nearby farming village.

Although they are different administrative villages under the Chinese system, Dora Karmo and Shamalang—along with another village, Serchukha—were traditionally part of the same community, Nanglangma. According to oral history, Nanglangma took its name from a lake in Pelyul County, close to where the original community was located before it moved to this part of Kham. At that time, the nomads believed in a folk religion, and, even now, its influences linger in daily religious practices. The local monastery for Nanglangma is Sengge Gonpa, a small monastery with little more than thirty monks, which belonged to the Nyingma sect of Tibetan Buddhism. It had close continuing links to the Derge Dzogchen monastery. Dorje Tashi, the local incarnate lama, had begun his monastic career in this monastery, and the monastery's leader was Dorje Tashi's close kin member. A network of familial connections linked this monastery with the communities it served. Sengge Gonpa itself, situated on the side of a mountain located at the far edge of Nanglangma's summer pastures amid a forest of fir trees, was located quite far from the winter pastures of Nanglangma and Dora Karmo.

— * —

One afternoon in spring, shortly after I had arrived, I went with Padka to herd the animals home for the evening. The lower half of her face was snugly covered in her pink scarf, and a long yak-hair slingshot, which Dora Karmo nomads use to crack the air or hurl stones at yaks when herding them, was tied around her waist. Padka was extremely adept with the sling, and I never ceased to be impressed by her accuracy and skill. We headed north up the valley, away from Taraka and in the general direction of Goroma, a neighboring nomadic community. As we walked, Padka pointed out landmarks. Immediately to our right was a small bump of a hill called Pozi Latse, adorned with prayer flags. This was a small local territorial deity, with whom some households had a good relationship. Behind Pozi Latse was the mountain of Zaka Megyal, a more powerful territorial deity. Looming above them both was the snow-covered form of Zhamo mountain, wife-mountain to the even-larger Zhara mountain located just a few kilometers north. Zhamo and Zhara were both very powerful and well-known territorial deities; monks and lamas chanted to them at certain rituals, and they were mentioned in history books of the Kham region of Tibet. The land and its features were living beings, animated with power and able to elicit actions and emotions in their relationships with each other and with nomads. For example, Zhara was believed to be the third son of the sacred mountain, Amnye Machen, located in the Amdo region of Tibet. His name literally means "can put," and it was said that, in looking for a special place to put his third son, Amnye Machen came across this area of Minyag and decided that he could put his son in this place. Zhara was a very powerful territorial deity and, in his jealousy over a supposed affair between Zhamo and Minyag Gungkar, had thrown a bolt of lightning at Zhamo, causing a jagged ridge to appear on her face. Through these narratives, Dora Karmo nomads cultivated and maintained active relationships with the different beings in their environment.

Padka had a slender yet strong frame. As we climbed farther away from both the pastures of Taraka and the foothills of Zhamo, she looked at me, panting slightly in the high altitude, and said, "Let's sit," then gracefully settled down on the slope of the mountain facing Zhamo. Like all Tibetan women, she sat with her knees together and feet pointing right and slightly backward. I was never comfortable in that position and sat cross-legged like a man, in spite of the folds of the *chuba* that I wore.

As I gazed at the mountain ahead of us, Padka gestured with her right hand, palm skyward and fingers together in a mark of respect.

"There is a beautiful lake there, Zhamo Yumtso. Do you know it?" she asked.

"No, I don't," I replied. "Is it big?"

"I don't know. Not as big as Ka Yumtso." Ka Yumtso, a larger lake below Zhamo Yumtso, was named after a small Bön monastery in the area. "There are many lakes in Dora Karmo," she added.

Eventually, I would climb to those foothills and admire the lakes for myself, clear pools of crystal waters fed by the melting snows of Zhamo mountain. In addition to those lakes, there was also Tso Talen, named after the saddlebags placed on horses, which the two small lakes resembled, and Rimtoma Tso, named after the small mountain that rose above it.

"Do you have lakes in your home?" Padka asked.

I looked uncomprehendingly at her.

She repeated, more slowly, "Do you have lakes in your home?"

Then I understood. My difficulty with their language was unsettling. It was not only their use of different words to convey objects and concepts that I thought were standard—"home," "children," "dog"—but also the accent and rapidity of their speech. Theirs was a thick and quick nomadic dialect that was unmodified for those unfamiliar with their speech, quite different from the clear speech that I was used to hearing from my Tibetan teachers, who, I realized, also modified their natural speech to accommodate my understanding. In those first few months in Dora Karmo, people did not modify their natural speech for me, and I was constantly taking notes on their words for certain objects and trying to keep up with their speech patterns. This was tedious work, not for me as much as for them because I was constantly asking questions. Padka, more than anyone, had been exceedingly patient and gracious in this regard.

She plucked a bright pink flower called *siter giter* (*Incarvillea compacta*, or dwarf hardy gloxinia) and then got up. From Padka, I would also learn about the flowers and plants in Dora Karmo. I followed her as we made our way back to the valley. We continued to walk for about half an hour,

Figure 2.1
View of lakes from Zaka hill, Dora Karmo, 2013. Photo by author.

crossing a small stream and passing a cluster of four winter houses in the distance. As we approached the animals from a wide arc, we saw another figure in the distance, coming from the opposite direction. Gyurmed Gonbo was a neighbor and kinsman. He was a short and sturdy man with a kind manner and crooked teeth. He was herding his animals back to his winter house as well and fell in step with us as we walked to the farthest animal and whistled it back.

"Are you tired?" he loudly greeted us.

"Not tired," we loudly replied.

We proceeded to walk back together. The animals of the two different herds were mixing, although, once or twice, Gyurmed Gonbo had to throw some stones at yaks that had taken to tussling with each other. Padka used her sling to crack the air and redirect wandering animals that strayed too far from the others. As neighbors and kinsmen, the households of Gatsong and Rachor interacted frequently, their animals grazed in the same spring pastures, and they moved collectively to the same summer pastures. As the cluster of winter houses came into sight, so did the fenced winter pastures.

Bordered by horizontal and vertical wires secured at regular intervals by round stays and supported by metal poles staked to the ground, these pastures were individual plots of land that no other household used, not even households of close kin. The size of these plots was assigned according to the number of people in a household. The division of land and fencing of pastures had taken place during the decollectivization period after 1980, under policies such as the Household Responsibility System and the Four That Form a Complete Set (the four being the fencing of pastures, construction of barns, construction of homes, and planting of small plots for hay). We passed a fenced pasture around the size of Gatsong's, and as we walked along the fence, Gyurmed Gonbo started to whistle at his animals and slowly walk away from us toward his winter house.

"Nyima Yangtso, come into the house, drink tea," he said to me.

I replied that I would go tomorrow as I caught up with Padka to help her lead all the animals into the enclosure of Gatsong's winter house for the evening.

That night, Panjur arrived in the house and stayed past dinner, which consisted of *tsampa* eaten with a wonderfully piquant cheese called *zhorshi*. I had never eaten it before and was later told that it was special not only to Kham but also to this particular area of Minyag and that its production was extremely labor-intensive. At this time, before his wedding to Padka, Panjur did not stay over regularly. Social custom dictated some distance between them, and, moreover, he was focused on gathering caterpillar fungus.

— * —

The first caterpillar-fungus-gathering excursion for that year occurred on April 11, or the thirteenth day of the second month according to the Tibetan calendar, when we were still living in the winter house. Caterpillar fungus is a particular hybrid of the larval and mycological, half caterpillar and half fungus. Its story begins when the larvae of a genus of moth are infected by the spores of a fungus (*Ophiocordyceps sinensis*). As the fungus develops, it parasitizes the caterpillar underground, eating it from the inside and simultaneously forcing the caterpillar into an upright position. After the caterpillar dies, the fungus sprouts a fruiting body. This stroma emerges from the head of the dead caterpillar and protrudes from the ground, similar in appearance to a small twig. Spores dispersed from this stroma can then infect other caterpillars, and the process continues.

Figure 2.2
Gatsong winter house, Dora Karmo, 2013. Photo by author.

The time-consuming task of gathering caterpillar fungus has increas-ingly drawn Tibetan nomads away from their usual herding activities because the price of dried caterpillar fungus is so high. As of 2013, the price per kilogram was more than that of gold, leading to similes compar-ing the situation to a Himalayan gold rush and the place to a Tibetan El Dorado. Wealthy Han from the eastern seaboard prize caterpillar fungus as a traditional Chinese medicine, and as China's wealth continues to rise, so, too, do the demand—and price—of commodities, such as caterpil-lar fungus. Many Tibetan nomads have gained different opportunities because of capitalist incursions into their lives. These incursions, with accompanying imaginaries of modernity, have the capacity to transform nomads' relationships with one another. Perhaps for the first time on the Tibetan plateau, stratification is occurring among nomads themselves. For some nomads, a desire for cash is accompanied by transformations in their relationships with entities of the physical environment, including yaks and territorial deities. While these kinds of transformations should not be viewed as "loss," in large part to avoid any romantic essentialism regarding "Tibet" and nomadism," there is some truth to the idea that the desire for cash comes at the expense of the relationships that fuel its creation, echoing anthropologist Anna Tsing's (2013) point that the power of capitalism feeds off *other* activities and networks that are not themselves regarded as "capitalistic" and are jeopardized as a result of this power.

Most nomads of Dora Karmo, however, were casual gatherers of caterpillar fungus—that is, they had not given up their animals and pastures to rely completely on income from fungus sales. For them, excursions to the foot of Zhamo mountain were also a social activity and an opportunity to meet with others in their immediate community. This is how I first met a number of people from neighboring households. Female casual gatherers would normally start to head up the mountain after the daily morning milking. Because springtime was hard on the animals, they did not produce much milk, and tasks associated with milking, such as churning butter or making cheese, did not take much time. In Gatsong, both Daka and Padka would often go up the mountain, usually returning with between five and ten fungi each. If there was too much other housework to do, only one sister would go. On one particular day early in the season, they both went. After rubbing butter, their high-altitude moisturizer, on their lips and hands to counter the drying effects of the harsh climate, they also, unusually, applied rouge to their cheeks and rebraided their hair before the day's outing.

We left the house and headed up toward the base of Zhamo mountain. After less than ten minutes, Padka started to walk away from us toward another part of the foothills. I followed Daka, who did not respond to my question about where Padka was going. I only later realized that Padka was going to meet Panjur, who had set up a white canvas tent, called a *gur* in Tibetan, in the foothills where he stayed the entire gathering season. The application of rouge to her cheeks suddenly made sense. As Daka and I proceeded, we met more and more people from neighboring households, some of whom were already familiar to me. Men, women, older men, and children were all part of our growing group. Some jokingly teased Daka about her new "friend"; others kindly asked me if I was well.

"Oh, are you the foreigner?" A man I had not met asked me after hearing that there was a foreign woman living in Gatsong.

Two women wandered up to join us but didn't speak.

He continued, "You look like an Amdo woman!"

I smiled and said, "No, no, I'm a foreigner. My home is far away, across a big ocean."

I assumed he thought I was from Amdo because of the way I tied my red belt. Moreover, I did not have red thread braided through my hair, unlike women from this area of Kham.

"You also speak differently," he said. "Like the literary speech. Our speech is very poor. I'm like a yak!" he continued.

During the entire walk, which was liberally peppered with breaks when we sat down in the pastures, an endless stream of questions came my way.

"Do you have caterpillar fungus in your home?" someone asked.

"No," I replied. "My home is a low place, and caterpillar fungus cannot grow there."

"What about yak?" the same person inquired.

"No yak," I replied. "But we have lots of sheep."

"Oh, like in Amdo. We had sheep here, too, but they died from a disease some time back. Now only Aku Niko has sheep. Isn't that right, Aku Niko?"

He continued: "What about horses? Are there horses in your home? And trees? What kind of trees? Fir trees like here? Is there grass? And rivers? And lakes? And snow mountains?"

I answered their questions, glad that I was able to fully understand them when they spoke to me, because, at this early stage, I still had difficulties with their natural speech among themselves.

They made appreciative clucking noises with their tongues when I told them that the seasons were upside down so that summer in Tibet was winter where I came from. In a characteristically Tibetan gesture, they quickly stuck out their tongues at every new fact or bit of information that surprised them. The hour or so that it took us to slowly walk to the places where they gathered caterpillar fungus was a good opportunity for me to introduce myself to the larger Dora Karmo community.

Finding caterpillar fungus was a singularly difficult task. The fungus protruded perpendicularly from the ground and looked like a small twig. A person identified it by placing his or her cheek on the ground and looking for the outline of the fungus against the rocks, grass, and bracken. Children, with their sharp eyes, were remarkably adept at finding the fungus. Caterpillar fungus tended to grow in the same area every year, so it helped to know the common breeding grounds. I was initially unable to identify the fungus even when the square meter of ground where it lay was pointed out to me. Eventually, my eyes became more attuned to the shape, color, and particular form of the fungus, but I never did find one entirely on my own.

On one of my ventures without any improvement in my ability to find the fungus, I lamented to Daka: "I can't do it, I can't see them if you don't help me. When did you start collecting the fungus?"

She replied, "When I was fifteen years old."

"Oh, so you have over fifteen years more experience than me!" I said.

She laughed. "Ho ho! Fifteen years more experience! Yes, I do."

I continued stooping to look at the ground.

Even though I was inept at collecting caterpillar fungus, I continued to accompany Daka and Padka because I, like everybody else, enjoyed the sociality of these excursions. The activity was the first opportunity to begin socializing again after a long and cold winter, during which all nomads stayed indoors and rarely saw others outside their immediate households. For young children, these excursions were a way of not only playing with one another but also contributing to household income. For younger people, spending time on the mountain and away from inquisitive eyes was a chance to flirt or rendezvous with potential suitors. For older nomads, the excursions allowed them the time and space to converse with one another and catch up on gossip.

— * —

The first move of the year, from the winter house to the black tent, occurred on a gray and snowy day at the end of May. The snow was uncharacteristic for this time of year, but the year had so far brought particularly bad weather. Rain and snow had fallen incessantly for three days. Except for going out to milk or herd the animals, the five of us remained indoors. As a result of this prolonged indoor dwelling, a kind of cabin fever had set in. I was feeling cold, dejected, and impatient to move. The dust in the room swirled around my headlamp. Over the course of those three long days, I checked and double-checked with Aku Kungo.

"When are we going to move?"

He replied, "On the fourth month, third day."

I didn't fully believe him. "You said we were going to move eight days ago."

He patiently said, "The weather was not good."

I doggedly persisted, "Then you said we were supposed to move yesterday."

He replied, "Jonla Kunchok said to wait."

"Now we move on the fourth month, third day?"

"Yes."

I did my approximate calculations—the third day of the fourth month was May 29. The next day.

On the morning of the move, Aku Kungo took his horse and a small red bucket of yogurt to Lhagang. He said that he wanted to give the yogurt to Dorje Tashi's mother. The wet and cold weather had turned the dry earth of the enclosed area outside the house into a gooey mass of mud. Padka and Tsering Panjur had left to take out the animals and prepare nine of the strongest load-bearing yaks for the move. In the house, the listlessness and unfocused energy of the past few days gave way to frenzy of activity. Daka was busy organizing bowls, pots, and cooking ingredients, such as salt, oil, chilies, and pickled vegetables. She told me to place them in plastic sacks. We would also move the old leather sacks of barley flour, wheat flour, and butter that had been stacked next to my bed all winter, although we were not going to carry all of them to the tent on this first move. Most would be transferred to the house of Jonla Kunchok so that, together with the sacks of six or seven other households, they could all be carried during the collective big move to the summer pastures the following month.

When Padka and Tsering Panjur returned with the yaks, they tied them in a single line along one straight rope fixed to the muddy ground. Daka shot off a list of instructions about which sacks should be taken first and how to load them onto the yaks: first the plastic sacks of pots, bowls, and provisions; then the wooden boxes of clothes and sacks of bedding; then the leather sacks of barley and wheat flour, rice and salt, and butter; then the long wooden poles; and, finally, the two heavy halves of the black tent itself. The six largest yaks were loaded up, their burdens tied to the wooden saddles with strings of strong old leather. Daka, Padka, Tsering, Panjur, and I walked the three hundred meters uphill to the fenced winter pasture with the six yaks that had been saddled with their loads. Inside the fenced pasture, we stopped next to six large, burned-looking stones. These would be used, as they had been in the past, to build the hearth. The yaks were unloaded beside the six stones. The last yak, carrying the heavy halves of the black tent, had wandered off, and Tsering Panjur ran to herd

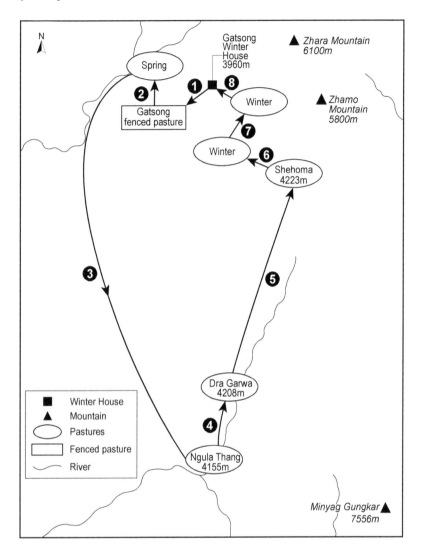

Figure 2.3
Diagram of pastoral movements (not to scale), 2006. Cartographer: Chandra Jayasuriya

it back. We unloaded the yaks and placed each half of the black tent on
either side of the items next to the stones. Each half of the tent consisted
of fifteen rectangles of cloth densely woven from yarn made by twisting
hair cut from the tails and sides of yaks. Tsering Panjur carried five of the

longest wooden poles and laid them on the ground between the halves of the tent. We attached the two halves together by looping the ends of ropes on one side, where they had been sewn along the inside of the tent, to their corresponding wooden pegs on the other side. These ropes are made from the soft down found on the undercoat of the yaks' bodies. As we worked, the snow gave way to a light drizzle.

Once the black tent was laid out correctly on the ground, Tsering Panjur wriggled beneath it, and, with Daka's help, he and Daka wedged the ropes into the grooved notch at the top of each pole and started to raise the poles, one by one, gradually inching them upright in a line until they raised the middle of the tent. Then we started to pull on the external ropes, creating tension by wedging the ropes onto the tops of the external poles and staking the ends of the ropes to the ground with wooden pegs. As we pulled the ropes over poles and staked them, nine per side, the black tent began to widen and rise off the ground like a giant black spider looming over the stones and provisions. We pulled the front and back of the tent in opposite directions, each supported by a pole, and staked the looped ends of the tent to the ground, creating more tension and height. Measured by the length of my boots, it was twenty-two boot lengths wide and twenty-four boot lengths deep.

The black yak-hair tent, however, was not merely a shelter from the elements. In many ways, it was a living entity that had to be tended. When it rained, the tent, while somewhat porous, retained moisture that weighed it down, causing it to droop and sag. We would then go out in the rain to lower the angle of the poles, releasing tension and reducing strain on the ropes and tent material. Under the strong sun of the grasslands, the tent dried, releasing moisture that sometimes rose in tendrils of steam. We would take turns lifting the tent by increasing the angle of the poles and tension of the ropes. Living in a black tent, one felt its subtle shifts in tension and weight distribution. We also tended the black tent in order to prolong its life and reduce wear and tear. Every autumn, nomad men spun the extra-long yarn—about ten meters per reel—that was used to make the densely woven yak-hair rectangles for the black tent. The rectangles measured about fifteen centimeters in width. Nomads removed one rectangle from the lowest sides of each half of the tent and sewed new rectangles onto the topmost sides of each half of the tent, regenerating the tent in an annual cycle of repair. With each half of the black tent composed of fifteen rectangles, the weather-worn, threadbare rectangles at the bottom of each half were fifteen years old.

Tent life was centered on the hearth. Between the second and third poles from the front, rectangular pieces of sod were cut and placed on top of one another beside the third pole, forming a ledge that would hold salt and other cooking provisions. Six burned-looking stones were placed upright and arranged in a rectangle, with two shared stones in the middle creating an upper and lower hearth. Pots rested on the tops of four stones. In the summer, with its long days, lush grass, and plentiful milk, the hearth was almost constantly in use. All morning, either Daka or Padka heated milk for churning butter and then heated the creamless milk to produce other dairy products. In the afternoon and evening, Daka used the hearth to boil water for tea and steamed wheat buns or dumplings called *momo*. The hearth was untended only when both Daka and Padka were busy with the animals, milking, herding, or gathering the one-year-old calves to be tied up for the evening.

Because their animals were so much a part of their lives and routine, it took me a while to appreciate how much the animals dictated the *way* of life for Dora Karmo nomads. The very pattern of their existence, moving from house to tent and from place to place within the tent, was premised on the needs of these animals. And while the strategy of the movements was deeply historical and practical, what emerged as well was the caring and intimate nature of the relationship between animal and human, in particular between lactating *dri* and nomad women. Every morning, Daka released the first yak calf from its evening separation and let it run to its mother. She called the mother with a three-syllable, imitative, grunting sound, *wo ae wog*, the first syllable high pitched, the second low pitched, and the third middle pitched. The sounds were placed before and after the animal's name, so a call for Karima sounded like "*wo ae wog*, Karima, *wo ae wog*." Sometimes only the lowest-pitch sound, *ae*, was tagged at the end: "*wo ae wog*, Karima, *ae ae*." The mother, recognizing the sound and her name, ran to Daka, expecting salt. The calf was sometimes allowed to suckle for a few seconds before Daka pulled it away and tied it to the portable wooden peg staked to the ground, just far enough away so it could not reach its mother. She tied the front legs of the mother together with her rope and knelt down next to its left side, facing the right hind leg.

Figure 2.4
Black tent at Shehoma, 2013. Photo by author.

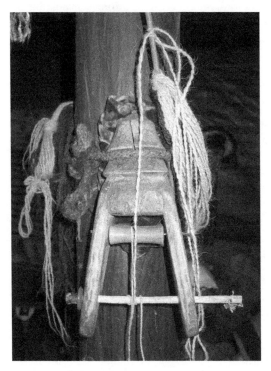

Figure 2.5
A Tibetan *tri* for spinning
yarn. Photo by author.

After reaching over and placing the wooden pail beneath the udder, she squeezed the teats alternately, squirting the milk into the pail. Sometimes the mother looked back and licked Daka's hair or back. Padka and I were pressed close to the sides of our own *dri*.

"Trika is difficult to milk," Padka said.

"Her teats are quite hard. I have to pull harder." Daka chimed in to say that sometimes Trika's two opposite teats gave more milk, so she preferred to milk those ones.

I listened in silence, focusing on my own animal and trying to aim the milk into the pail and not onto the ground.

"Nyima Yangtso, is it hard?" Daka laughed at me. "Got any milk yet, hoh ho!"

I persevered and replied, "A little!"

She laughed again. "Hoh, we'll give you the easy ones to milk!"

The intimacy between women and *dri* included care for baby calves. It was not uncommon for nomad women to give particular attention to sick calves, and, if necessary, a woman would carry a sick calf on her back during the main move to the summer pasture. The level of care was in keeping with their practical instinct to maintain as many animals as possible for their livelihood. But it also indicated an emotional instinct to preserve life. Once, in late spring, a calf was born in the middle of the night. The baby was born weak and, by morning, had not yet learned to stand or suckle. Padka carried it inside, sat down by the hearth, and placed it on her lap. Its umbilical cord was still attached, and though the blood and birthing fluids had dried on its fur, it was still slightly damp. She held it close to her to keep it warm and wiped its face with a dirty green rag. Daka had started to warm up some milk on the hearth. When it was warm, she poured it into a bowl and gave it to Padka. Padka drew a mouthful of milk. With her left hand, she turned up the calf's head, gently pried open the calf's mouth with her right index finger, and waited until it started to suck her finger. Then slowly, she lowered her head and placed her mouth onto the calf's mouth, dribbling in milk. The calf suckled a bowl of milk, and Padka fed it in this way for five days. Unfortunately, the calf did not survive. Padka alone fed the calf this way, which I later came to realize was not common practice beyond this particular household. Padka's specific compassion toward animals was yet another aspect of her character that I came to appreciate and love. To me, it became clear that the way she related to and treated animals reflected how she related to me and other humans.

— * —

The black tent had a rhythm in the wind. The tent sides swayed or flapped according to the intensity of the wind, and these syncopated sounds enveloped life in the tent. Inside the tent, light filtered in as either a swath of blinding white through the open top flap or a gray paucity struggling through the gaps of tightly woven yak hair.

We stayed in the spring pastures for another three weeks before Jonla Kunchok, in consultation with the stars and monks at Sengge monastery, said it would soon be time to move to Ngulathang, the summer pastures of Nanglangma. This was a big move and took two days for many households, who would move all their belongings and the black tent on the first day and then move their herds on the second.

Just before this move, Aku Kungo suggested that we ride to Lhagang. He said that he needed to go to the hospital for medicine [although I later learned that he went to see his brother, a Tibetan medical doctor] and told me to buy whatever I needed —fruits, candy, paper—to prepare for life in Ngulathang. Once there, it would not be convenient for me to leave. He himself would stay in the winter house because he was old, and with Panjur around, he was not needed in the summer pasture. We saddled the horses and rode slowly to Lhagang. Making our way up the hill called Azoma and cautiously crossing the dirt road from Lhagang, we remained silent for the first half of the journey. After we reached the bumpy grasslands and settled into the ride that brought us alongside streams and meadows of wildflowers, Aku Kungo and I resumed an ongoing thread of conversation about the changes in Dora Karmo. I was deeply interested in his thoughts on the developments in the area, brought about not only by the activities of Dorje Tashi, the local incarnate lama, but also by an American development organization. The organization had wanted to involve Dora Karmo nomads in its efforts to create a participatory comanagement system of grasslands, which included designating the area as a nature reserve in order to protect it from poaching and other illegal acts. Aku Kungo had previously been reticent on the subject of these international development initiatives, but he spoke at length during this part of the ride.

"We asked for saddles and guns so that we could patrol the area," he said. "But the organization said that it could not give us guns because that was against the law. And it didn't see how saddles would help with environmental patrols. Instead, it said it could give us binoculars so that we could *see* the poachers."

Aku Kungo smiled to himself, and I laughed aloud at the thought.

"Did the organization give the binoculars?" I asked him.

"Yes, yes. They are in Aku Dorje's* house now," he remarked quietly.

"What do you think about the organization's work? Is it bringing good change to Dora Karmo?"

There was a brief silence as our horses made their way across a rocky stream.

"They came in the winter last year, with many Chinese workers and workers from Amdo who talked a lot. We didn't really understand them. But we were asked about our problems. 'You tell us your problems, what is most important, what is less important,' they said to us. And the workers wrote [the problems] down and put numbers next to them. Then they gave everyone some paper and told us to write down which number was the most important problem. And then less important and less important. Even the children and old women!"

At this point, he chuckled heartily to himself.

"Children and old women! They don't know how to write or read! So they said to others, 'You write for me.'"

"There were some important problems," Aku Kungo continued. "We wanted electricity. And a road, because we wanted to go to Lhagang more quickly. But the organization said this was the government's job, and it couldn't do the government's work. So, then, the leaders wrote a letter to ask for guns. And, well, I've told you what happened."

The conversation trailed off. Within two hours of our departure, we were on the dusty main street of Lhagang. Unaccustomed to the noise, cars, and people after two months in the pastures, I briefly followed Aku Kungo around the shops in a slight daze. Then he told me to visit Tashi's family. The house, previously so familiar, seemed particularly grand and colorful—opulent, even. Tashi's parents greeted me warmly and remarked how dark I had become while offering bowls of tea, food, and fruit. They were concerned about how difficult life must be and wondered about my health and happiness. I insisted that I was very well and that the household, Gatsong, was very good to me. They laughed as I spoke, saying that I was beginning to sound and look like a *drogmo*, a nomad woman. I was warmed by their familiarity and concern, realizing that all my energy in the past few months had been devoted to the novel and strange: learning the vernacular of Dora Karmo nomads, becoming physically conditioned to a cold and difficult environment, and joining in new activities, such as milking, churning butter, and making yarn. It was comforting to sit on something other than the ground, to speak in a dialect that I readily understood, and to eat fruit. The hour passed quickly.

I had told Aku Kungo I would meet him by the horses. As I left, Ala Lhamo, Tashi's mother, held my hands and said that if it was too difficult, I could always come back to their house. Her face was full of concern. I was deeply touched but also resolved to stick to my plans.

I replied with lightness in my voice and a smile, "But I'm a nomad woman now."

CHAPTER 3

Life in the Summer Pasture

The shared summer pastures of Nanglangma are called **Ngulathang.** More than a hundred years ago, when the nomads of Nanglangma first came to this area, Ngulathang was the site of their winter pastures. The name, which means "**Crying Grasslands,**" is related to a story about Aku Dretung, uncle to Ling Gesar, eastern Tibet's mythic-historical king. Aku Dretung was on his way to Dartsedo when he passed through a vast place that was full of trees and rocks. It was covered with thick fog, and he lost his way. For three days, he wandered, lost, hungry, and cold. Finally, in despair, he lamented to the gods and cried for help in finding a way out. The gods took pity on his tears and cleared the fog.

Even though most of the trees had been cleared because of external and local logging activities, the whole area was still marked by large rocks and stones, which were often named as places and landmarks of shared significance. Large and prominent stone formations marked not only the topography of the area but also, practically, the way between the villages of Nanglangma and toward their respective winter pastures. Some stone formations had meanings attached to them, based on particular shapes or peculiarities. The entire area—characterized by small and large rocks on the ground, dense patchy coverings of rhododendron and potentilla shrubs, and large tracts of sodden bumpy grasslands—was widely regarded as tough terrain for both humans and animals.

After we arrived in the usual place where the household, Gatsong, pitched its black tent for the first time in Ngulathang, Padka and Tsering Panjur argued about exactly where to place the entry to the tent.

"These are the hearth stones from last year. We should have the door close to them," Panjur said.

"Yes, but we should also move the hearth so that the grass can grow back there. And last year, the ground was uneven in that place," Padka replied.

"What about moving over there?" asked Panjur, pointing to the left.

"Then we are directly below Ani Moko's tent. There are too many stones there, and it will be difficult to tie down the tent," Padka patiently replied. "How about to the right, and then we are slightly closer to the water?" she added.

Panjur grumbled slightly under his breath. "The slope is much steeper there. It will be hard to sleep."

"Well," Padka said finally, "we can move the tent slightly higher up. Over there." She pointed to a fairly wide patch of lush long grass, dotted with small yellow flowers called *katsa metog* (*Ranunculus japonicus*). These small buttercups were so named because of their spicy taste.

"Ya ya, that's good," Panjur replied.

They were debating over a fairly restricted space, since there were already three other tents pitched around them and the rest of the area was covered with rocks and shrubs.

The tent was quickly pitched, but it was not fully set up until Daka arrived the following afternoon with all the animals and other household items. She had spent the night in a white summer tent less than two kilometers away because of a decree issued by the community leader, Aku Kunchok. The arrival of animals into Ngulathang had to be staggered over a few days so as to avoid mixing the herds with unfamiliar others and therefore minimizing fighting among the male animals. Yaks fighting yaks often resulted in people fighting people. In the morning, Padka and Tsering Panjur rode to help Daka. They arrived back in the black tent, which was then arranged according to the template. Looking in from the entrance, there was a single rope stretched vertically to the right. It had twenty evenly spaced loops, each to be attached to a wooden toggle on a baby yak's collar. The baby yaks slept there every evening, their presence warming the tent. In the middle section of the tent were five hearth stones, located in the lower half of the tent, and an altar was placed in the top half. To the left of the stove was the family area. Here, in the lowest part beside the tent flap, dried branches of *sera*, a kind of rhododendron, formed a meter-high wall that provided both kindling for the yak dung fire and protection from gusts of wind. Padka and Tsering Panjur's clothes and bedding were put away beside it. Pots, buckets, the butter-churning machine, and other kitchen items were located slightly above this, and, still farther up, Daka's clothes and bedding were neatly folded and put aside. I had been given the respected sleeping position beside the altar and sacks of *tsampa*, salt, and food items. My bed was composed of neatly arranged dried branches on which I placed my sleeping mat, sleeping bag, and backpack.

The three surrounding tents in this place belonged to kin members from Aku Kungo's side of the family. Ani Moko was his paternal first cousin, a large woman in her early fifties with a broad and generous smile that revealed a set of even, white teeth. She lived in a black tent with her husband, Aku Gyurmed. Her oldest daughter, Chomo, lived in a neighboring black tent with her husband and a three-year-old daughter. The third black tent belonged to Aku Lhorda and Ani Lhabko, although Aku Lhorda chose to remain in the winter pasture in their winter house. Aku Lhorda was Ani Moko's older brother. Three other kin-related households lived on an opposite northwesterly hill across a fifty-meter-wide hollow of rocks and white- and yellow-flowered shrubs. Gyurmed Gonbo was Ani Moko's younger brother. He had married Chonyi Wangmo and moved into her household as a *magpa*, or called-in son-in-law, just like Tsering Panjur. Their house was called Rachor. Aga was also Ani Moko's younger brother, and he had married Tsetse. Ani Moko, Aku Lhorda, Gyurmed Gonbo, and Aga were all from one father and mother. For Tibetans, those denoted as coming from one father and mother had the closest of kinship ties in a general context in which a person often had multiple half siblings. In addition, there were an older brother who was a monk and a scholar at Minzu University in Beijing and a younger brother who was also a monk and living in Tsongon. With slightly more than 180 households in both villages of Dora Karmo, everyone was kin-related, making for a tight-knit community. Following the Tibetan adage of *mi rab dun*, or seven generations, by which one acknowledges seven generations of kin relations, the obligation both supports requests for help from these cousins and prohibits marriage between such cousins. In practice, with regional movements and lack of birth records, one can realistically trace back only four or five generations.

In this place, the black tent of Gatsong faced northwest with the impressive face of Zhara mountain to its right. On a clear day, at the slightly higher elevation of 4,200 meters, one could make out the colorful prayer flags that marked the hill called Chenresig in Lhagang town. And in the early dawn, after the women rose to release the baby yaks and milk the female yaks, the cascades of mist that almost always hung over the grasslands would gradually lift to reveal the hint of town life in the distance. Spirals of smoke indicated there, as in Ngulathang, that households had woken from the night's slumber.

For Tibetan nomad women, summer mornings were long and busy. After they were done with the morning milking, it was imperative to immediately heat large steel pots of milk so that they could churn the milk into butter. Butter was made using one of the ubiquitous yellow churning machines manufactured in Qinghai. The churner had to be assembled before each use and cleaned and disassembled afterward. Before the machine came to Dora Karmo in the early 1990s, nomads churned butter the traditional way, with two women each using a long wooden paddle to beat the milk. Old women still reminisced about the old method, fondly recalling the good smell of butter being churned in this way. They added that there was no smell with the machines, although the quality of the butter was comparable.

Nevertheless, the butter-churning machine was convenient because the work could be done by one person, and the other could lead out the animals for the day. The milk was first heated on the yak dung fire until it just reached the boiling point. If the milk boiled over and sizzled on the hot stones, creating a splatter of ash and smoke in the tent, the woman tending the pot would add cold milk to stem the boiling. In Dora Karmo, she would also place some juniper branches on the stones where milk had spilled and quickly recite *mani* chants. The general practice of cleansing by way of juniper smoke is found all over the Minyag area. After the milk was adequately heated, the woman poured it through a piece of cheesecloth draped over the holding bowl or receptacle at the top of the butter-churning machine.

Because of the high fat content of the milk (about 5–7%), it was not necessary to let it sit in order to separate the cream. Instead, churning the hot milk produced a thick cream that slowly trickled down one end of the butter churner to a small pot. The cream was left overnight to settle, although sometimes two days passed before it hardened and could be patted into butter, a process that produced very little buttermilk. After the hot milk had been churned and the cream separated, the woman reheated the leftover skim milk, called *dara*, in the large pot and poured a souring agent derived from yak stomach out of a big bucket into the pot to curdle the milk. The result was a type of cottage cheese. While it was fresh, the cheese was reheated, then pulled and molded with a ladle into a braid of stringy cheese called *api*. *Api* lasts for a few days, and nomads tear off strings of it to eat with *tsampa*. When the cheese was not made into *api*, it was spread out on a blue tarpaulin under the hot summer sun and left to dry. In its dried form, it was called *chura* and could be kept for many months, providing additional nutrition during the cold and milk-limited winter.

Nomad women also made yogurt, or *zho*. In Dora Karmo, yogurt was made only occasionally because it required whole milk and therefore affected the amount of butter that the household could produce and store. To make yogurt, a woman placed a portion of hot milk in a small wooden bucket and added yogurt starter, which she stirred into the milk with a small twig or branch. She then wrapped the bucket in various pieces of clothing or blankets so that it would keep warm overnight. By the next morning, the yogurt had usually curdled sufficiently. It had to be consumed within a few days, and during that time a new batch had to be made with the old yogurt as starter. Yogurt starter often circulated throughout the community, with women constantly going back and forth between households to request a little bowl of starter when needed. Such visits were also the perfect excuse for stopping in at neighboring households and staying for a cup of tea and news.

In performing their various household tasks, women invariably synchronized their early morning movements, from lighting the first fire to milking animals and churning butter. After the milk had been churned into butter, four women emerged from their respective black tents with identical bronze ladles tucked between their necks and right shoulders. They bent over to tip the water in the ladles into their cupped hands, which they washed quickly under the steady stream. When their hands were clean, they returned to their tents to pat the butter into large rounds

FIGURE 3.1
Inside a black tent, Dora Karmo, 2006. Photo by author.

and then stored them in fresh water. With the plentiful supply of milk in summer, this particular synchronized routine of preparing to pat butter occurred every two days or so.

Daily tasks took all morning to complete, so it was usually only in the early afternoon, when the sun was high and the black tent at times unbearably hot, that the women had some time to themselves and with their young children. In the afternoons, the women had more time to socialize with neighbors and would often visit one another in their respective tents. It is important to note that these women and children were close kin to the household because, as Robert Ekvall has rightly noted about the social customs of Tibetan nomads, "visiting is not casual" ([1968] 1983, 74). When I lived in Gatsong, Ani Moko was a frequent visitor to the black tent and was usually invited to have tea and *tsampa*.

"Come in, Ani Moko, come in! Are you tired?" Daka exclaimed while on her way to grab some dried yak dung for the fire.

"No, no," Ani Moko heaved a reply as she placed her granddaughter on the ground and settled her own large frame across from the hearth stones.

Then looking directly at me, she asked, "Ya, is it difficult?" At that time, I had not had many occasions to speak with Ani Moko and was still slightly unsure of how she was related to the household.

"No, not difficult," I replied.

Ani Moko looked at Daka and said, "She speaks Tibetan."

Daka chuckled slightly. "Yes, she speaks Tibetan! Don't you, Nyima Yangtso?!"

I sensed a slight teasing in her voice and merely smiled in reply.

Ani Moko asked, "Is that her name? Nyima Yangtso? Who gave you the name?" She addressed me directly.

"Zenkar Rinpoche," I replied.

"Hoh! Zenkar Rinpoche is number one!" She nodded approvingly, shaking her thumb in an upright gesture.

Ani Moko paused, not sure of what else she could say to me or that I would understand.

"Is our nomad life difficult?" she finally asked.

"No, I don't think so," I replied. "But I cannot wake up every morning at five like Daka and Padka to milk the animals! I'm not a good worker." Then to Daka, I added, "Sorry," because I had felt sorry that I was not as hardy.

"Hoh, hoh! 'Not a good worker,'" Ani Moko parroted. I realized that I still did not speak like them even though I was gaining more confidence in my ability to understand their natural speech.

Then, losing interest, Ani Moko turned to Daka and said, "Aku fell off his horse yesterday and hurt his leg, ho!"

Daka asked if he was all right.

"He'll be all right! But his pride won't be! He's at home looking after his leg, and Tashi [his son] has gone to Sengge monastery to ask the lamas for some medicine. Tashi wanted to go to Lhagang to buy the medicine, but Aku wanted Tibetan medicine from the monastery, so Tashi went."

She turned to me again and asked loudly, "Eh, Nyima Yangtso! Do you know how to ride a horse?"

Daka answered on my behalf. "She rode to Zaka yesterday! And she rode back by herself."

Zaka was the hermitage of Aku Zhiko, a revered old lama in the area.

"Aku Zhiko is a good lama and a very good fortune-teller," Ani Moko said, and then to me, "Did you ask him for a divination?"

"No," I replied from where I was now sitting on my sleeping mat, "but I will!"

"Ai, Lhamo, what are you doing?" Ani Moko exclaimed to her small three-year-old granddaughter, who had picked up a knife she had found. The child's face crumpled into an impending wail when Daka suddenly called out to the front of the tent, pretending someone was outside, "Oh, what do you want? Lhamo? But she's busy crying. When she stops, I'll let you know, but she's crying a lot so don't wait!"

At these words, the little girl immediately looked up and toddled to the tent entrance. With a potential tantrum averted, Ani Moko and Daka sat talking for a little while longer.

"Did you see Tsomo's new coral? It's really large and beautiful, but it doesn't look real," Ani Moko said.

"I saw her the other day when I was in Lhagang. Where did she get it?" Daka murmured in reply.

"Do [Dartsedo] perhaps. You can buy all sorts of things there these days," Ani Moko continued. "But it was a present, it is said. Because how could Dorje afford it? Even with the caterpillar fungus money, they still have to pay for Ani's hospital fees. And then they have to pay for the children's school fees."

"Who gave it to her?" Daka asked.

"I don't know," Ani Moko replied.

"Perhaps Dorje did some other work? He was working on the road a few years ago," Daka added.

"Perhaps, or perhaps she has . . ." Ani Moko trailed off and then turned to glance at me. I was following the conversation with interest even though I was, by now, hunched over my notebook and seated slightly apart from them.

There was a moment's silence before Ani Moko said loudly, "Well, I'm going."

"Stay, Ani Moko, have more tea," Daka urged.

"No, I have *chura* to dry," Ani Moko replied while getting up. She walked up to me and looked at my notebook, and then at the pen in my left hand.

"Tch, tch, using her left hand," she said. She was referring to a Tibetan custom of using primarily the right hand for everything from kneading *tsampa* dough to performing ritual actions. These small details again set me apart from them. As she left, Ani Moko said to me with an encouraging smile, "Eh, Nyima Yangtso, come and visit us!"

"Oh ya, Ani Moko. I will come tomorrow or the day after," I said.

She walked out with her heavy gait, holding Lhamo's hand. As always after she left, the tent felt silent and bereft without her large, hearty presence.

When I lived in Gatsong, the daughters of Aku Gyurmed Gonbo and Ani Chonyi Wangmo, from Rachor household, often visited. The three girls—Pelma Lhaka, Wonam Drolma, and Pelma Tso—were sixteen years, thirteen years, and nine years old. This was according to Tibetan reckoning, which counted the time in the womb as one year. In Western calculations, they were each a year younger. Pelma Tso, especially, had developed a fondness for me after the times we had played together in the school courtyard when I first arrived in Dora Karmo. She was a sweet, quiet girl who was happy to hold my hand and take me places when the adults told her to. Several times, Padka had joked with me and asked if I wanted to take Pelma Tso home when I left them. I always replied that I thought she would miss her parents too much, but I wondered what the future was for this young girl. Would she grow up to be a nomad wife and mother like those around her?

During these summer days, we would pat butter in the evenings, placing the freshly made rounds into buckets of icy spring water that provided natural refrigeration over those warmer months. The most important milk product of Dora Karmo nomads, butter played an important role in the daily diet and in ritual offerings and acts. Because butter production was dependent on the amount of milk and, in particular, on the household's surplus milk, wealthier households that had greater numbers of *dri* were able to produce more butter and to use it more readily and freely. In mid-July, at the height of the summer season, the household Gatsong produced roughly 5 *jin*,[1] or 3 kilograms, of butter a day. Milk and butter production reached its peak in August, when butter production was about 6 *jin*, or 3.5 kilograms, a day. This was the amount of butter produced in a household with about forty milking animals.

---

1   One *jin*, a common Chinese unit of measure for weight, is roughly equivalent to 600 grams.

As food, butter was mainly added to tea, to form the basis for *tsampa*, the main staple of the Tibetan diet. Unlike neighboring sedentary agriculturalists and nomadic pastoralists in other Tibetan areas, Dora Karmo nomads did not drink butter tea, which was made in a long wooden cylinder. Instead, they drank milk tea and gave butter to monasteries for the monks to consume and as offering for the monastery's ritual practices, such as creating butter sculptures and lighting butter lamps. Dora Karmo nomads traded with Tibetan agriculturalists for the Tibetan staple *nei*, or barley. Butter was the main product used by Dora Karmo nomads in their trade with sedentary agriculturalists, and in 2006 market prices or exchange ratios, an equal weight of butter was worth up to eight times more than an equal weight of *nei*. In Dora Karmo, trade with Tibetan farmers was generally conducted in Lhagang town or in more distant Rangaka. Most Dora Karmo households roasted *nei* and ground it outside the fenced house area of Jonla Kunchok, which had a water-powered stone mill.

By far, the most labor-intensive and delicious milk product made in Dora Karmo was *zhorshi*, a full-fat Tibetan cheese. It could be either quite liquid (summer *zhorshi*) or hard (winter *zhorshi*). Making *zhorshi* requires a skilled hand, and Daka generously allowed me to help her on more than one occasion.

"Here, Nyima Yangtso, cut these [branches] to this length," she instructed, pointing toward the willow shrub called *langma* (*Salix thamsoni*).

While I did that, she cut and stripped the bark off the pliable branches, revealing a bone-white interior.

"We have to cut the branches in the fourth month. Otherwise the milk will not 'stick' to the branches and we can't make *zhorshi*," Daka explained.

She placed the branches in the wooden buckets that she used for milking and for making yogurt. After that, she and Padka milked directly into the wooden buckets lined with *langma* branches. At the end of each morning, they poured out the milk as usual into large pots. During the first few weeks or so, the process merely "treated" the branches, and nothing observable occurred. Eventually, however, residual milk began to stick to the branches until it built up and formed a spongy coating on the branches.

This is the initial stage of producing *zhorshi*. After about a month, enough milk had stuck to the branches that it was time for Daka to collect the white and spongy coating and place it into a heavy-bottomed pot.

"Nyima Yangtso, put more dried yak dung into the fire," she instructed me. The spongy coating had to be boiled for one to two hours. I watched the fire diligently. As the coating boiled, it began to thicken. A piquant smell filled the black tent. When the substance was sufficiently reduced, Daka took the pot off the stove and immediately placed the *zhorshi* in a jar to cool. Summer *zhorshi* remained fairly runny through the heating and storing process. Everyone loved eating it with *tsampa*, and it was usually brought out for only the most respected and welcome guests.

As the summer progressed and the *langma* branches had been through several rounds of *zhorshi* making, Dora Karmo nomads made another type of *zhorshi*. The process remained the same: milking into and pouring the milk out of the wooden bucket until the residual milk built up to form a spongy coating on the branches. The longer the *langma* branches were used, the more quickly the buildup occurred. After around two weeks, a significant amount of milk had stuck to the branches.

To make winter *zhorshi*, Daka repeated the process of collecting the spongy coating from the branches, placing it in the pot, and boiling it for a few hours. This time, the final product was a darker beige. After it had cooled, she placed this *zhorshi* in a prepared yak calf stomach, where the rennet curdled the milk and created the winter *zhorshi*. We ate this cheese several months later after it had become brown-gray and developed a nutty flavor and firm texture. I loved winter *zhorshi* more than its summer variant. When placed over the stove and heated, it reminded me of grilled haloumi.

For the most part, the household itself consumed the *zhorshi*. When plentiful, it was the highlight of the evening meal, which was also the most social time for the household itself. Because everyone was usually busy with their respective tasks during the day, members of the household shared any news they had heard over the course of the day at the evening meal. During summer, this meal was always prepared and cooked in the dark because the longer days brought a correspondingly longer workday. Animals were herded back and tied up later than in the winter. When the last baby animals had been tied up, Daka returned to the black tent and connected the plug on the solar panel to the single lightbulb hanging from the fourth pole from the entrance. Electric light shone for less than an hour in the evening, but it helped her prepare the evening meal. In nomadic areas, casual visitors never visited during this last meal, so it was also an opportunity for everyone in the household to catch up on the latest gossip about their neighbors. In a close-knit society, stories spread by word of mouth.

In this household, Tsering Panjur usually had a wealth of outside information to share. As a nomad man, he was not tied to the tent and the animals in the way that Daka and Padka were. Many of his responsibilities, such as cutting wood, collecting herbal plants and flowers, selling yak meat, and buying provisions such as flour and salt, necessitated leaving the immediate area around the tent and interacting more widely with households from other villages and people in Lhagang and Rangaka towns. His motorcycle, purchased the previous year with caterpillar fungus money, also allowed him to cover more distance in less time and more often than before. After his travels to Lhagang and Rangaka, especially, he would return to the tent and, in the glow of the yak dung fire, tell us dinnertime stories about the latest fight in Lhagang, about how a Han man had died while hiking alone around Zhara mountain, about the highest prices of caterpillar fungus and rumors of middlemen making hundreds of thousands of dollars in Dartsedo, about the newest items on sale in these towns, and so on. Yet Panjur's stories were neither quite as interesting nor told with as much detail and finesse as the stories related by his father, Aku Thubten. Aku Thubten was from a farming village around Rangaka, and perhaps because of this, his speech was immediately familiar to me. His manner was naturally performative.

Sometime before we had left the spring pasture for Ngulathang, Aku Thubten visited Gatsong. "*Khaliy, khaliy, khaliy!*" Aku Kungo said enthusiastically as Aku Thubten dismounted his horse and brushed his *chuba* vigorously with its long sleeves.

"Drink some tea, sit there," Aku Kungo offered as he limped back to his felt sitting mat, high on the right side of the hearth.

"Oh ya," said Aku Thubten, sitting down with a flourish on a guest mat, placed slightly below Aku Kungo and toward the front entrance.

"Many people in town [Lhagang]?" Aku Kungo asked.

The increased number of tourists in Lhagang was the subject of many conversations among Dora Karmo nomads, not least because the main highlight for these mostly Han tours was Dorje Tashi's impressive golden stupa complex. Dorje Tashi was an influential and wealthy local lama who had a tumultuous relationship with residents of Lhagang. A number of residents did not like him, even though they benefited economically from many of his projects, including the welfare school and golden stupa complex. Dorje Tashi was a kin member of Dora Karmo, and many nomads in Dora Karmo thought that these Lhagang townsfolk had gained an economic advantage at Dorje Tashi's expense despite saying unfavorable things about him. This caused local tensions between some Lhagang residents and Dora Karmo nomads.

"Haiiii!" Aku Thubten replied to Aku Kungo's inquiry while shaking his head. "There were big busloads! You know those buses that carry more than twenty or thirty people. There were maybe ten of these in town, but mainly at the golden stupa. Chinese everywhere! Then there were some private cars, not government cars, but wealthy Chinese families. The cars were big, black. I heard that one of them costs more than 500,000 *gurmo*.[2] But on the black market, without papers, you can buy one for 100,000 *gurmo*."

At this point, Aku Kungo shook his head while clicking his tongue. "What's so good about them?" he asked.

Aku Thubten replied, "I heard you don't have to drive them. You can just hold the wheel and turn it left or right. Then to stop the car, you press down with your foot, and it stops right away. And the cars have phones in them and also televisions! But I don't know how they get electricity in the car. Do you know?" Aku Thubten turned inquiringly to Aku Kungo.

"I don't know!" Aku Kungo replied with a smile, again shaking his head.

Aku Thubten pondered this while taking a big gulp of tea and then said, "Peh, many of the Chinese rode horses. Fifty dollars for not even twenty minutes! They (Lhagang villagers) are making so much money. They only walk up and down Drolma hill with the Chinese; it's easy work! It is said that Rinchen made up to 1,000 *gurmo* in a day. I believe it, after the number of Chinese I saw. If each bus has more than twenty people and there are ten buses, then it must be true, mustn't it?"

2   Dora Karmo nomads expressed these amounts as *gurmo*, the Tibetan word for "money," which is not a monetary unit.

He paused to seek confirmation from Aku Kungo, who just shook his head and said, "Ya, drink tea."

Aku Thubten took a sip and continued. "Ho ho, there is a lot of money in Lhagang these days. The businessmen get rich from the Chinese and caterpillar fungus. The monks all have mobile phones, and they are planning to build a new monastery gate and new rooms for the monks. It is said that the American foundation is going to help."

At this stage, he looked at me, but I kept silent because I didn't know whether or not this information was correct.

Aku Thubten took another gulp of tea and continued on a different topic, this time related to local affairs. "Peh, the scum Palzang* is going to take more for himself. How can ¥90,000 just go missing? Of course he knew what happened to it. Township government money is meant for the whole township, not one government office or one person. But the office buys big cars and the governor buys a new apartment in Dartsedo—¥90,000, almost ¥100,000. Pi!" He shook his head in disgust. He sat cross-legged and did not gesticulate much. The power of his speech was in his voice and the remarkable modulations he achieved at the beginning, middle, and end of sentences.

"Ya, drink tea," Aku Kungo said calmly, as always. He stayed silent. Aku Kungo was not a big talker in any setting. He spoke only of what he knew directly, and because he didn't travel to Lhagang as frequently as others, he rarely contributed to the topics of conversation that nomad men mostly talked about: money, horses, motorcycles and other vehicles, caterpillar fungus, and material developments in towns. He did have clear and respected thoughts on education, religious affairs, and traditional medicine, the last because his younger brother was a Tibetan medical doctor in Lhagang and his maternal uncle was a well-known Tibetan medicine specialist at Jango monastery in nearby Goroma village. His devotion to Buddhist teachings and practices, his solid foundation in Tibetan language and culture, and his clear love of, and pride in, a pastoralist way of life framed the values of his household. They had been transmitted to his daughters—in particular, Padka—and, in some way, had influenced my understanding of the community and what I would eventually focus on in further research. The household members' persistent commitment to a pastoralist way of life despite the lure of alternatives made possible by caterpillar fungus money, their continued practice of rituals and religious offerings, their broad understanding of the environment mainly because so many of their kin relatives were Tibetan medical specialists, and their deep respect for religious figures were revealed in stark relief when compared with other households in Dora Karmo.

Panjur's recent arrival to the household had added new elements to their way of life. Since he was much younger, eight years younger than Padka, and able to come and go from the house, he interacted enthusiastically with the new things and ideas he encountered in town. Buoyed by newly acquired wealth from caterpillar fungus sales, he often bought things that he thought would make life easier in the home, such as manufactured ropes with winches and multifunction pocket knives, eagerly displaying them to Aku Kungo and Padka with a salesmanlike narrative of how useful the things were. Personal objects, such as a mobile phone and a leather jacket, also caught his fancy, but his performance over such items was more discreet, embarrassed even. They would emerge only when Padka asked him if he had bought anything in town and would be quickly put away under a pile of other things. During his first year of living in the Gatsong household, Panjur purchased two major items that typified the desires and situation of young nomad men in Kham: a motorcycle and a horse. He bought the former for around ¥3,000 and it was his primary means of travel between places in Dora Karmo and from Dora Karmo to Lhagang and Rangaka. A motorcycle was called an "iron horse" in Dora Karmo, and it was regarded as both necessary and convenient. However, for most men, it was neither a status symbol nor an object in which they took particular pride.

Panjur purchased his horse slightly later, and it cost almost ¥5,000. It was a lovely chestnut called Jonra. Panjur was clearly proud of the animal and had ridden it to his own wedding ceremony with Padka. He would not ride it for household activities and chose another steed if the weather was inclement. But he would interact with it every day, either by whistling when it was time for it to be fed with a bowl of *tsampa* mixed with milk washings, which is what he fed the two dogs of the household, or walking over to give it a pat and some kind words. A Tibetan nomad male will scour available resources to purchase particularly fine steeds and usually continually upgrades his mount, if possible. He attaches markers beyond considerations of financial value to a fine horse: it is an extension of himself and his prowess. He will groom and adorn the animal with great diligence and care, often placing it above all other animals and possessions. While we were in Ngulathang, Panjur began to groom the animal more carefully and ride it to places near the black tent. He started to treat the horse's leather straps with butter, which kept them supple and gave them a dark shine. This was in preparation for an annual event that was greatly anticipated by the entire community of Nanglangma: the summer horse festival.

— * —

On the twentieth day of the sixth month of the Fire-Dog year 2133, the four villages of Nanglangma held their annual summer horse festival in the summer pastures of Shamalang, adjacent to the forested valley where Sengge monastery was located. Each year, the villages took turns hosting the festival. In Gatsong, morning milking proceeded as usual. Because Padka stayed behind, Daka and I did not have to tend to the milk, and we left shortly after ten in the morning with Ani Moko and other women and children from the neighboring tents. Panjur had left the day before to perform *ri bog shung*, a ritual act offering payment to a territorial deity for leasing hills and mountains and using the things that grow there. That day, Panjur traveled to a local territorial deity called Kera Amu to perform a *sang*, or smoke-purification, ritual as payment. This ritual consisted of combining butter and *tsampa* and burning the mixture with juniper branches. The smoke was thought not only to appease the territorial deity and thus any powers that it could confer on the ritual supplicant but also to purify the deity itself. The smoke offering was accompanied by standard ritual chants to ordinary deities or specific chants to more powerful deities. Panjur spent the afternoon at Kera Amu and then rode to the festival site to stay the night with his parents and younger sister in the Shamalang summer pastures.

We rode for more than an hour to the site of the festivities. The summer horse festival was the high point of the social calendar. Daka and Lhadron, Ani Moko's younger daughter, had taken the trouble to put rouge on their cheeks and wear fine clothes. As we approached the main festival area, I noticed that a number of decorated white summer tents had been put up; the black yak-hair tents of Shamalang were farther away. We walked toward the main festival tent, which was five times the size of the others. The excitement in the air was tangible. Ani Moko, Daka, and their friends enthusiastically called out to friends and relatives.

"Ai Tsemo! When did you arrive? We just got here, going to Bamu's tent! See you at the race?"

"Oh, Lhamo, yes, yes, we will come over to see you later. When? Before the race? Ya!"

"Oh, look at that new robe, Daka! I saw it in town the other day. From Lhasa, and what a color! But it's too expensive, more than 200 *gurmo* per meter. Oh, but it looks good!"

As the women talked excitedly among themselves and with others, I took in the atmosphere of the horse festival, noting that tourists and other foreigners had not yet found this event because it was set back from the main road. Nomads from the other villages barely noticed me, and their casual acceptance made me feel like I was part of the community. I remained silent as we walked toward the main festival tent for a religious teaching and sat on the ground with the other nomad men, women, and children. The head incarnate lama of Lithang monastery was seated on a raised dais about fifty meters away, flanked by monks on both sides and at his feet. He was talking about the importance of the environment for nomads, in both practical and religious terms, and about protecting wildlife in the area. But as I was trying to understand what he was saying, children ran around, asking for plastic-wrapped candy and distributing handfuls of dried sunflower seeds. Nomads sat in attentive stillness, apart from skillfully moving their front teeth to crack the husks of sunflower seeds while their tongues whisked away the kernel within.

Horse festivals occur at various times during the year across the Tibetan plateau. Nomads celebrate the Tibetan new year with such festivities, although the festival occurs less frequently in the winter months when the ground is hardened by ice and snow. By far, the largest and most significant horse festivals occur during the summer, in the bull (fifth) and tiger (sixth) months of the Tibetan calendar. The horse festival is important for a variety of reasons, not least because the horse holds a special place in the history and culture of Tibet, particularly among Tibetan nomads. In monetary terms, a handsome animal can fetch up to ¥20,000 in some nomadic areas of Amdo and Kham.

In Tibetan history, the mount of Ling Gesar, the famous warrior-king of eastern Tibet, to which the nomads of Dora Karmo are regionally linked, is a deity who reincarnates as a steed named Kyang Go Karkar. He aids Ling Gesar in his battles against demons, delusions, and ignorance.

Alexandra David-Neel, after traveling extensively through Eastern Tibet in the 1920s and 1930s, wrote that "by further order of the Precious Guru and the gods, a race must be organized in which all horsemen, whoever they may be, young or old, servants, beggars or sons of good family, shall be allowed to take part without exception. The first who will arrive at the throne, placed as winning post, and sit on it shall be proclaimed King of Ling, the treasures that he will discover at Magyalpumra shall become his exclusive property, and Tampgyaltsen shall give him his daughter in marriage" (David-Neel and Lama Yongden 1978, 123–24).

Traditionally, horse festivals marked the time when nomads gathered to celebrate summer in a tribute to mountain deities on the "four victories of the month of the bull" and when the elders of the community met to discuss pasture management and coordinate decrees. According to Namkhai Norbu Rinpoche, horse festivals also occurred at the important gathering of the tiger month, from the fifth to the tenth day of the sixth month in the Tibetan calendar, another occasion when elders discussed issues of common interest, including how to avenge blood feuds and raid enemy villages. On both these occasions, the dates of which differ from community to community, the horse festival displayed the fighting abilities of the young men, valorizing their skills on horseback through contests of speed, agility, and precision. Whereas Namkhai Norbu Rinpoche observed contests of dexterity involving "gathering the flower in one's mouth" and "picking the tip of the flower" in his travels in eastern Tibet in the 1950s, the tests of fifty years ago had changed to gathering white *khata*, or ceremonial scarves, from the ground while riding a galloping horse. Groups of riders representing their various villages and marked by different colors of shirts took turns performing the tests after the main race was run. It was a time for young Tibetan men to instate themselves within the community as potential heroes and warriors and for established heroes and warriors to maintain their skills. It was also an opportunity for the relatively isolated villages and communities to come together.

This abiding sense of community purpose was evident in the Nanglangma horse festival. The horse festivals of Lhagang and Goroma village appear to have lost their original community purpose, transformed into performances for tourists and other visitors. Nonetheless, the summer horse festival of Nanglangma retained a semblance of its original functions.

FIGURE 3.2
Nanglangma horse festival, Ngulathang, 2013. Photo by author.

For the main race in the Nanglangma horse festival, nomads dispersed along most of the course of the race. In that year, approximately one hundred horses participated in the main horse-racing event, and around thirty prizes were given out. The prizes ranged from packets of cigarettes to boxes of tea. The main race took about five minutes to complete, and it was difficult to view the entire race clearly because of the distance involved. Despite this, older people sitting in front of me were calling out names as the race progressed, correctly identifying the winner, at a distance of almost two kilometers, as a young nomad man from Serchukha village. The holder of second place was a young man from Shamalang. In third place—could it be?—the old men next to us weren't sure. Daka looked on excitedly as others identified the person she thought it was: Panjur! I looked questioningly at Daka once I realized, and she laughed to confirm. We sat happily in silence, observing the rest of the race, which lasted only a few more minutes. When it was over, the crowd got up to walk slowly to their tents, talk about the race, and meet up with the winners. After a while, I became separated from Daka and then decided to wander by myself to the flat expanse of ground where the displays of horse-riding prowess were going to take place.

People had already gathered around the opposite sides of the expanse and along its length. A *latse*, or cairn, at one end marked the territory of the territorial deity called Drubja. On the other end, an impressive vista opened to a view of Zhara mountain. The excitement rose as more and more people came and sat on the ground along the length of the space. The displays would be held close to the crowd, whereas the main race had seemed far away and somewhat removed. As young men started to ride from one end to the other, throwing themselves spectacularly from one side to another of their galloping horses, we could feel the thundering hooves on the ground. People became more animated, cheering the representatives of their villages and laughing when a rider made a small mistake or failed to pick up a *khata* from the ground. A few other foreigners mingled with the crowd—apparently, the race was close enough to the main road and open to tourists seeking to "gaze at the exotic other" (Urry 2002).

That year, the gaze was subjected to unanticipated manipulation. The staff of an international development organization had been invited by Shamalang village elders and were treated as guests of honor. After the displays were finished, a performance had been prepared back at the main tent. The village elders placed the Lithang monastery incarnate lama in the prime seat, a row of monks sat on carpets on the ground beneath him, and members of the development organization were placed on both sides of the monks. The village elders ceremoniously presented the monks and guests with white scarves and bottled drinks. Then they brought in an amplifier and a generator, and a nomad woman, one of the few who attended the workshops organized by the international organization, spoke through a microphone and welcomed everyone to the festival. A series of songs and dances and a skit were performed, but only for the guests, because all the performances were turned toward them, and the nomad audience saw only the backs of the performers. Nonetheless, the nomad audience saw the incarnate lama, monks, and members of the international organization as if they were on display. The Shamalang village elders had orchestrated two levels of performance, to show the nomads from other villages their special relationship with the wealthy foreigners and to publicly place the members of the international organization in a position of reciprocity with Shamalang village.

At the end of the performances, Daka and the rest of the women got up to leave the festival site. It was already late afternoon, and even though the festival was still buzzing, the women had to return to the black tents, animals, and children. On our way through the throngs of people and white festival tents, we bumped into Panjur, happily carrying bricks of tea under his arm.

"Ai, Panjur, careful you don't break your arm," Ani Moko teased.

He smiled broadly and gave the bricks of tea to Daka, who wrapped them in the folds of her Tibetan robe.

He looked at me and smiled proudly while saying, "Ride back safely, Nyima Yangtso! Don't race home!"

Given my relative unease on horseback, this wasn't likely, but I cheerfully replied, "Only if Daka does!"

We picked our way back, although it was difficult to go slowly because the horses had caught the mood of the festival as well and were full of energy. By the time we reached the black tent, though, the festival itself seemed far away. Padka was eager to hear all the news and gossip and was particularly happy about Panjur's win. She smiled to herself as she put away the bricks of tea and then went about her usual work.

— * —

Padka's full name was Padka Lhamo. She was born in the year of the Horse and said that she was particularly fond of horses for that reason. As far as I could tell, she was fond of all animals. Out of all the people in the household, she was the one who spent the most time with the animals— milking the *dri*, taking the herd out to pasture in the morning and bringing it back in the evening, tending to ill creatures and nurturing weak ones. Padka was a gentle and kind person who was compassionate toward not only human beings but also every living being. She was also the first to make me feel that I was a functioning part of the household, giving me little jobs to do, teaching me how to crack a yak-hair slingshot and spin yak hair, and taking the trouble to help me learn their vernacular. She had studied for two years in primary school, she told me, and had learned how to write her name as well as a few other words in Tibetan. She still had a crumpled copy of a primary school Tibetan-language textbook among her belongings.

"I had wanted to become a Tibetan medicine doctor, just like my uncle, but I couldn't stay in school because I had to work in the house. I had to help Daka," she added.

In hindsight, I realized that this departure from study coincided with the unexplained disappearance of her older sister and the death of her mother.

"But I do know a little about Tibetan medicine from my uncle," she continued. "About the flowers and plants, mainly. I know a bit about their names, and when to collect them, and what they are good for. I also know a little about how to treat animals if they are sick."

There was a small measure of pride in her quiet manner.

Padka had never been east of Dora Karmo, toward the prefectural seat, Dartsedo, and large Chinese cities. Three years before, she had traveled west to Lhasa with her father and oldest sister, a trip she said she would never forget. Daka had remained at home to look after the animals, her own travel taking her to Dartsedo to stay with a relative for a few months. The trip to Lhasa lasted a month, and they traveled north via Qinghai. It was a pilgrimage, and she felt particularly moved by the statue of the Lhasa Jowo, which local people in this area believe is integrally connected to the statue of the Lhagang Jowo in the Lhagang monastery. A few years later, she traveled with Panjur to the holy site of Larung Gar, where the renowned treasure revealer Gyurmed Phuntsog had established a Buddhist teaching college for monks and nuns.

We were working together, spreading out cheese on the blue tarpaulin so that it would dry under the blazing summer sun. During the mostly sunny summer days, it was more bearable to be outside and to feel the cool breeze of the high mountain air. The black tent could feel like a furnace inside, and not only because of the summer sun. During days of heavy rain, the top flap of the tent would be closed, but the yak dung fire still had to be stoked for daily household chores, and the smoke in the tent was often overpowering. Padka laughed, recalling a recent afternoon when Daka had closed the top flap of the black tent while stoking the fire with wood. The smoke was so intense and sharp that it had sent me and a few visiting children running outside with tears in our eyes.

"Yak dung smoke is not painful," she said.

"No, it is not as painful as wood smoke," I agreed.

Padka and I worked together often in Ngulathang, and I sought out her company, even though my labor was mostly not needed. Since she did the majority of the female work outside the black tent, such as herding and gathering mushrooms and tubers, her work was generally more physically demanding than Daka's tasks, which were focused on the stove and were done inside and around the black tent.

One day, after leading out the animals, Padka and I continued walking toward a forested area known as Karchag. It was full of evergreen fir trees that also provided the ideal environment for mushrooms, both edible and poisonous. Padka showed me a remarkable variety, pointing out golden coral mushrooms and large wood ears. Their names in the vernacular were descriptive and imaginative: birds' hands, horses' hooves, madness mushroom, and old woman's spindle. As we walked farther and farther into the forest, I asked Padka nervously if she knew the way.

"Don't worry, Achi Nyima," she replied. "Pay attention to the sun."

She crept deftly under low branches and jumped over large tree roots. Then suddenly, she stopped and raised her hand. I immediately stopped as well and looked inquiringly at her.

After a few long moments, she laughed, albeit nervously. "Let's walk this other way," she said.

"What is it?" I asked as we walked downhill.

She looked at me. "A wolves' lair" she said. Then, when she saw my face, she added, "But don't worry! They aren't here during the day."

We made our way quickly and quietly, and after we had reached the southern edge of the forest, Padka turned to me and said, "I was so scared, Achi Nyima! My heart went *da da da*." She thumped her chest and laughed nervously.

"Well, I'm glad you didn't show it!" I replied, now fully realizing how dangerous the situation could have been. "I'm so glad it is OK!" I added, belatedly feeling the fear she had felt earlier.

"Oh! Let's sit down," Padka said, still giggling nervously. She reached out and broke off several stalks of *karyang*, a kind of rhubarb that is refreshing to eat despite being immensely sour. She gave me a few stalks, which resembled a combination of rhubarb and celery, before peeling off the outer layers of those she had kept for herself and eating them.

"Our Tibetan apple," she said between mouth-puckering chews.

It was difficult not to screw up my mouth because the stalks were so sour, and so delicious!

"Here we say that this plant is, at first, like a heart because of the shape of the bud amid its leaves. Then it is like horns because it comes up from the ground like horns. Finally, it is like a lama because of its yellow stalk against its red leaves. At this time, in the autumn, it doesn't taste good."

Padka broke off a few more stalks from the numerous *karyang* plants in the area and secured them under her belt at her lower back. She carried these home for Daka.

Padka was pregnant. She was due to give birth in the late autumn, but three months before her due date, she was barely showing a bump through the folds of her long Tibetan robe. She also continued to work as she had before. Her due date was less than nine months after her wedding to Panjur, making it apparent that they had consummated the union before any official and public ceremony. They had spent much time in each other's company during the caterpillar-fungus-gathering season the previous year.

Padka's quiet but friendly manner made her generally well liked and popular. Panjur counted himself fortunate that his feelings were reciprocated. In addition, there had been considerations for the household because of Aku Kungo's advancing years. Daka had committed herself to a life of celibacy. She had initially wanted to be a nun but had remained to look after the household instead. The household needed a called-in son-in-law, both because it could not afford to lose Padka's labor and because it needed a younger man to take over the tasks that Aku Kungo was increasingly unable to do. The fact that Panjur was from Shamalang, which was part of Nanglangma and the home village of Aku Kungo's wife, was another point in his favor.

Padka and Panjur had an easygoing manner with each other. In those early months of their married life together, they often went out to herd the animals or work together. It was the only time they could be alone with each other. When they returned to the house, Panjur occasionally had flowers in his long hair or Padka usually carried a small bunch of wildflowers that she immediately placed on the altar. Their manner with each other imparted a natural ease to a household that had otherwise grown from three to five adults in the space of less than three months.

— * —

By the end of our sojourn in Ngulathang, I had been living with the household and community for almost five months. While I had made strides in my comprehension of their natural speech and had started to feel habituated to life in Gatsong, there also had been moments, particularly when visitors were present, that I felt left out of their conversations and shared joviality. A few times, I felt slightly irritated, as, for instance, when more distant relatives or friends came to the tent and the first thing they said after exchanging initial greetings with either Daka or Padka was "Not Chinese?" while looking at me. My irritation stemmed from knowing that nomads do not regard Han people well and thinking that, since I was taking the trouble to learn their language and way of life, *surely* it was apparent that I was *not* a Han person! As I had learned from my initial year in Gudrah town, because of my upbringing in a distinctly Malaysian home, I did not feel much in common with Han people from China.

Another instance of genuine discomfort stood out for me. This occurred when there was an unusually large gathering—of around seven women and children—in the black tent while we were still in the spring pastures. Daka and Padka were busy pouring tea and offering *tsampa* when a piece of *tsampa* hit my right shoulder. I never figured out if it was an accidental or purposeful act, or who had done it, but I felt selfishly affronted that no one seemed to realize how difficult it sometimes was to be living there, with no space of my own and my every action subject to scrutiny and general comment.

Yet the fact that my every action was scrutinized and then presented for public knowledge also opened up possibilities for shared merriment. This revolved mainly around my inability to perform certain tasks or how I confused or misunderstood certain words but included more than that. Embedded in Daka's or Panjur's telling of these kinds of stories to Ani Moko, and anyone else who was visiting the black tent at the time, was their way of giving me a place in their lives. I was sure of this and glad for the general feeling of goodwill created by the laughter that accompanied these stories. One story involved my particular interaction with a *dzomo*, or hybrid cow-yak, named Galuh. Galuh was the only *dzomo* in the herd and around four years old at the time. She was much more independent and clever than the others. For example, whenever the animals were herded back to the tent in the evenings, Galuh would always lead them in because she would then be the first to drink the leftover liquid from the cheese-making process. She would also be the first to come toward us when we tied up the baby yaks in the black tent for the evening because she would get to lick the most salt from our fingers. Because I was always chasing her away from the tent (she would enter looking for salt) or away from the wooden tent poles where she liked to scratch her head, I developed an affection for her. Her distinct black-and-white markings also made her stand out from the herd's uniform black.

One evening, after we had all retired to sleep, Galuh entered the black tent through its front flap, looking for salt. Apparently, she did this often, but that evening, she wandered up to the top of the tent where I was sleeping, right next to the large bag of salt. The subsequent moments were hazy for me because I was in a deep sleep until I felt a large, rough tongue, lick my right ear and then slurp horizontally across my face. I awoke more fully to the cries of Daka, shouting at Galuh, "Go away! Away!"

A hoof stepped on the kindling that made up the base of my bed and then I felt the thuds of scuttling hooves as the animal ran out of the tent.

"Nyima Yangtso, Nyima Yangtso,'" Daka called to me, "are you OK?"

"Yes, I'm fine," I replied. In fact, I was so tired and confused that I merely wiped my face and went back to sleep.

The next morning, after I had risen from my sleeping bag and dressed, Padka came into the tent with a bucket full of milk and laughter in her eyes when she saw me.

"How did you sleep?" she asked merrily.

"Haha, fine," I said.

Then while we were all having second morning tea, I recounted my memory of the evening and was happy when I made them hoot with laughter, particularly at the description of Galuh's tongue across my face.

"Did she really lick you?" Daka asked incredulously.

"Yes!" I replied and made a sweeping motion with my right palm across my face. Padka held her sides, while Daka leaned forward with laughter.

They told this story to everyone who visited the tent for the next few weeks, and I was encouraged to recount my version, too. The story did much, I believe, to include me in their personal and social lives, particularly because their initial impressions of me were shaped by *un*familiarity despite my projection as a person familiar with Tibetan culture and language and who knew religious figures and intellectuals.

This realization was brought home to me only much later. Their early hesitation during conversations when I was present, and occasional hostility to me as a person, had much to do with my unfamiliarity, both as a person and as a *kind* of person. Even though I wore Tibetan clothes, I never wore them in quite the same way that they did. My hair was not braided in red and black wool, wrapped around my head, and decorated with large rounds of ivory resin just above my ears. My hands were always much cleaner than theirs despite months without a bath. My hiking boots were relatively clunky, and they never stopped commenting on how large my feet were for a skinny person. Initially, as well, I am sure that they thought of me as a government official or international development *kind* of person (because for many pastoralists, local government officials and Tibetan development workers were of the same kind). On another level, I looked like a Han but said I was a foreigner, which made me similar to the many Chinese disciples of their incarnate lama Dorje Tashi who came from Hong Kong, Taiwan, Malaysia, and Singapore. Moreover, by actively referring to Dorje Tashi and Zenkar Rinpoche, I must have reinforced this particular impression. Finally, my familiarity with Tibetan language was specific both to the standard language of my interlocutors at the Sichuan Province Tibetan School and to a certain kind of terminology. My lack of fluency in their natural speech, particularly in the early months, must have added more interpersonal confusion than if I was completely mute and uncomprehending. For most of this period of my formal fieldwork, they never really knew when I would understand them either directly or in conversation with others. And I myself could not foresee when some conversations would be crystal-clear and others a frustrating struggle to understand.

This collective aspect of living with others who were radically different was integral to my fieldwork experience and to my appreciation of ethnography because it laid the foundation for those shared moments that result from living together and being able to draw on this repository of shared experiences. It helped me slowly adapt not only my own perceptions of myself but also, through my effort to understand them, our relationship with one another. Even though the ideas of fieldwork and ethnography initially contributed to the complex of resources that I drew on to help sustain myself in the field, these ideas eventually gave way to more personal resources as I began to relate with Dora Karmo nomads as people and not as research subjects or repositories of research information. However, accepting the conditions of unfamiliarity also entailed exposing my sense of self.

CHAPTER 4

A World of Impermanence

As I became more involved in the rhythms of daily life in Gatsong, I recalled the first time I entered the black tent of a Tibetan nomad family. It was July 2003. I was in Sershul (Ch. Shiqu) County, about a thousand kilometers northwest of Dartsedo town, with one of my closest Tibetan friends, Perlo. We left the county town at dawn to travel an uncomfortable hour by motorbike to the pastures of the Sershul summer horse festival. The horse festival was in its fourth day and approaching the end of celebrations. We stayed through the morning and observed several displays of equestrian prowess: male nomads swooping down to pick up white *khata* with their horses at a full gallop. Observers whooped in delight at their skill amid the danger. Perlo and I had gone there to meet one of his cousins, who had agreed to let me stay in his black tent in their summer pasture for a week. This was an experience that I was equally excited and nervous about: I would be there completely on my own, as Perlo had to return to the county seat for work. My language, while passable, was oriented toward a farming dialect; most of the nomadic speech in this area was unintelligible to me. And to top it off, the family tent was a six-hour horse ride away, taking me far away from anything familiar.

The journey did not begin well. The horse I mounted immediately galloped off at full pace. I clung on while Perlo's cousin rushed after me on his own horse. When he finally brought the horses to a canter, we turned back toward Perlo and the small group that had gathered as soon as they had seen a foreign woman gallop off on an overly energetic horse.

"Are you OK?" Perlo asked in English.

"Yes, yes, I'm fine," I replied.

He smiled and said by way of apology, "The horses are very active because of the horse festival."

Others in the group appeared to commend me for not getting thrown off. I was slightly shaken and asked for a gentler ride, which I received. Despite my mellow new horse, the ride to the summer pastures of Deshungma was uncomfortable and difficult. I had not eaten a proper breakfast and felt light-headed by the time we took our first rest, about two hours into the journey. At this point, we had left the signs of civilization behind and were sitting on a wide ridge that marked an approach to another high valley. We had not brought any food, and Perlo was concerned.

"It is maybe another hour or so until we reach some black tents. We can get some tea there," he told me. I mustered a small smile and said that I was fine.

It was another two hours before our first black tent came into view, and I felt weak. The woman in the black tent knew Perlo's cousin and greeted us warmly. Nevertheless, as we sat in her black tent drinking milk tea, I had an increasing sense of foreboding. I asked Perlo how much longer we had to travel. Two more hours. I pressed him on whether he had to return that evening or could stay at least one night. He had to return right away because of a meeting the very next day. The grasslands in this region are vast, and at an average altitude of more than 4,500 meters, they are seriously remote. As these thoughts played out in my mind, I started to feel short of breath.

I turned to him worriedly and said, "I'm not feeling well."

He looked at me calmly and said, "Maybe you need some fresh air. Let's go outside."

The sun was dazzling and the air was sharp, even in July.

I said to him, "I don't think I can go on. I'm feeling sick."

He looked searchingly at me. "But you have never had a problem with altitude sickness. Is it your body or your mind?"

I looked down at the grass and the small blue flowers. "I have never felt like this in a Tibetan area, but I am scared. After you leave, I will be all alone, and I can't communicate well with your cousin, and we are so far away from Dzachukha [town]. I can't stay here by myself."

Perlo looked at me with compassion and replied, "OK, then we will go back now."

"I'm sorry," I said to him, feeling terrible.

"Don't be sorry," he replied. "This is not the right time for you. I hope that in the future you can come back here. It is a special place."

As he returned to the black tent to tell his cousin about the change in plans, I looked around with sorrow and regret. It was such a beautiful place, and I felt tiny and insignificant, both physically and emotionally, for not being able to persist within it. We saddled the horses, and when I realized that Perlo's cousin would have to return with us because neither Perlo nor I knew the way back, I felt even worse. It was a miserable ride back to Dzachukha town despite the good spirits of my traveling companions.

When we arrived, we had been on horseback for close to ten hours. Perlo's cousin left us just outside town to return to the summer pasture. I was exhausted, sore, and famished. But even as I settled into bed after gulping down a bowl of noodles, I knew in the back of my mind that this experience, this failure, was an important lesson. On reflection, it introduced me to the power of feeling overwhelmed by a vast and remote landscape, feelings that I would later learn to control. Eventually, I would even welcome this landscape and seek refuge in it. The incident also exposed my anxiety about being completely dependent on strangers, not only for the means of physical sustenance but also for company and conversation. Even during my weakest and loneliest moments in Dora Karmo, remembering this experience would give me the resolve and fortitude to carry on.

— * —

After thirty-five days in Ngulathang, we moved to the summer pastures by Dra Garwa, the stone formation known for the clicking sound reminiscent of a blacksmith's hammer. We had different neighbors, as Ani Moko and Chomo set up their tents in a new location. Directly above Gatsong were the black tents of Aku Kungo's fraternal nephew and niece. Tsering was the son of Aku Kungo's older brother, who lived in Lhagang town and was a Tibetan medicine doctor, and his younger sister, Wangmo, was two years younger than Daka. They seemed quiet and serious, with none of the jokes and guffaws I now associated with Ani Moko on her visits to the tent. There was something clearly dependable about their manner, and Daka and Padka held them in high esteem. We stayed in Dra Garwa for another fifteen days and then moved to the autumn pastures, located at the base of Zhamo mountain. This pattern of movement was the same from year to year, even to the exact location in a particular pasture, except when animal illness either required the herds of certain households to be placed in isolation or limited animal mobility. Decisions on these matters, as well as the timing of moves, were made by Jonla Kunchok, the village leader, in consultation with Sengge monastery monks and with reference to the traditional Tibetan calendar. The initial energy and excitement of the first few moves had been replaced by the routine of knowing our respective responsibilities in the process of packing, moving, and unpacking. Daka no longer had to tell us what to do. We all moved instinctively, each performing our tasks almost habitually.

By the time we reached Shehoma, the autumn pastures for the household Gatsong, most of the vibrant spring and summer flowers had died off and the sun was at an evening slant that bathed the grasslands in a warm golden light. Zhamo mountain, its snow melted into the streams and rivers that sustained the community, revealed a stark face. Even the permanent ice field at its peak seemed slightly diminished. In this place, if one squinted hard enough at the base of the mountain, one could make out the mounds of stone hermitage houses—scores of them—that had been the silent meditation retreats of many previous lamas. Locals said that more than a thousand years ago, a Kagyu sect monastery had stood in place of these stone mounds. They did not know how it was destroyed but insisted that it had been there and that this explained why there was not a Kagyu sect monastery in the entire area of Lhagang. From Shehoma, the winter house of Gatsong was now a half-hour walk toward the valley. We made occasional visits to Aku Kungo in order to bring him a fresh round of butter or a small plastic bottle of milk.

As the days became shorter, so did the workday for Daka and Padka. There was also noticeably less milk to boil, churn, and convert into storable products such as butter and cheese. Panjur busied himself with collecting herbal medicines from the base of Zhamo mountain, beside the hill associated with another territorial deity known as Zaka Megyal. Autumn was the best season for collecting edible tubers, known as *droma*, as well as a range of medicinal flowers and edible mushrooms. The riches of summer had to be consumed quickly in order to fortify the body for the long and harsh Tibetan winter.

By this time, Padka and Panjur had begun to share stories with me in

FIGURE 4.1
Daka and a baby
yak. Photo by
author.

a way that made me feel like part of the household. Daka, by nature more reserved, was still relaxed with me only when we worked together. During these times, however, we communicated easily. A breakthrough moment occurred close to the winter pastures one autumn afternoon after we had completed the morning's tasks. That day, Daka and I went to cut and collect *nyerma*, a tall shrub that grew in thick clusters and had a purplish-red tinge to its small leaves. She carried a sickle-shaped knife and walked toward the fenced winter pastures of Jonla.

As we crawled between the wires of the fence, I asked her uncertainly, "Is it OK to come in here?"

She laughed and replied, "Make sure they don't see us!" and continued walking slightly uphill to where the *nyerma* had grown thickest and bushiest with the summer sun and rain.

As she started to vigorously prune the shrub, I looked over my shoulder somewhat nervously, expecting to see Woje Tashi or Aku Kunchok coming to scold us.

Daka saw my nervousness and said, "Don't worry!"

I wandered over to help her arrange the meter-high cuttings into a bunch.

As the bunch grew bigger and bigger, I said to her, "More? Surely that's enough! It's too big; you can't carry all that!"

"Yes, more," she replied. "Can you carry some, too?" she asked, her eyes twinkling with challenge.

"Yes, but not that much!" I answered.

"Ho ho, not that much," she echoed, mimicking my speech. "A little bit, then," she added. She then started to make another bunch of cuttings, far smaller than hers.

As we tied the very large bunch of *nyerma* together with old leather straps, I said to her again, "It's really big. Are you sure you can carry this?"

"Ya. Can you carry yours?"

"Ya."

She helped me first, placing the bunch upright and holding it steady while I sat on the ground and harnessed it on my shoulders with the leather strap, like a backpack. It was difficult standing up with the bunch of cuttings limiting my forward movement, but I managed, rather ungracefully, to get to my feet. Now I had to help her. The bunch of cuttings she had gathered was double her girth. Even holding it upright and steady was difficult, and as she sat on the ground, running the leather straps around her shoulders and waist, I wondered how she was going to sit up.

On her first attempt, she came crashing back down again.

"Ho ho, ah, uh oh," she guffawed.

I couldn't help but laugh with her, at the sight of a woman, shorter than I was, supporting a massive bunch of cuttings twice her height on her back and hips. On her second attempt, rolling sideways onto one knee and then, with my help, onto her opposite foot, she managed to stand upright and remain steady. Then, with a big grunt, she bent forward and started to walk, still bent forward, with her burden bouncing in rhythm to her gait. I had my own burden, and even with its far smaller size, I had difficulty matching the rhythm of its bounce to my gait.

"Nyima Yangtso, lean forward," Daka cried out.

I leaned forward and walking immediately became easier, although balance then became an issue. I tried to focus and not laugh or stop concentrating on combining balance, forward motion, backward-leaning load, and uphill slope. Oh dear! The fence—how on earth would we pass? We walked along it until we came to a spot where the ground was slightly raised and the fence slightly depressed. This had been done before. Pressing the wire down with all my might, I helped Daka get over and then scrambled over while she helped me. We puffed our way back to the black tent, where we arranged bunches of *nyerma* at the front to block the wind. From this time, Daka became more accepting of my presence in their household, which manifested in her giving me more instructions on what to do and being more patient when replying to my questions.

During our time in the summer pastures, Aku Kungo remained in the winter house. For a number of days in the autumn, however, he walked to Shehoma and spent the day in the black tent, spinning yak hair into extra-long yarn for black tent repairs and carving wood into toggles for the year-old yak calves that had now grown big and strong. One day, Aku Kungo came to the black tent early in the morning. There was to be a ritual for some of the animals that would "free" their lives. This meant they could not be killed, herded, or used in any way. In addition, one of them was to be named and given to, Norlha Dzamba, a god of wealth. Pelma Tso came to the tent that day as well. Her family's black tent, quite far from Gatsong's in Dra Garwa, was set up closer in Shehoma. She arrived as the household was busy preparing for the ritual and helped whenever she was asked.

The revered Shanba lama performed the ritual, which consisted of chanting a specific ritual text while doing a smoke-purification offering. Shanba lama arrived in the late morning on horseback with a servant monk. He walked slowly into the black tent, where special cushions had been laid out for him and the altar items meticulously cleaned. He had brought juniper branches from Zaka Megyal hill, said to be particularly fragrant and efficacious for smoke-purification offerings. The entire household was in a flurry of activity: Daka to make fresh tea and a fried braided dough called *go re* for the honored guests, Padka and Panjur to assemble the appropriate animals for the ritual, and Aku Kungo to ensure that everything went smoothly. Even Pelma Tso was given little instructions and tasks. After months of feeling familiar and having a routine, I was suddenly a stranger again and an observer of their activities. I hung back, not knowing what to do.

Shanba lama placed the special juniper branches on the hot hearth rocks. Then he walked with Aku Kungo toward the animals. The six animals who were to figure in the ritual had been tied up so that they could not follow the rest of the herd as it was led out to graze. Shanba lama walked among the animals while chanting under his breath. In the meantime, Pelma Tso brought out a small metal urn filled with smoking juniper branches. This was the basis of the smoke offering. Shanba lama chanted, and the six animals became god-yaks, or *lha yag*, of the herd. As god-yaks, they could not be tied or tagged, which distinguished them from the rest of the herd. These animals were free to graze, although all usually stayed with the herd. When they were with the others, they were not herded by means of whistling or being struck with a stone. Further injunctions included not cutting their hair and fur, not using them to carry loads, and not killing them, although their carcasses could be used once they died.

After a while, Shanba lama pointed to a black-and-white two-year-old with no horns. This animal was separated from the remaining five and led aside. Aku Kungo cut some tufts of hair from the animal's head and chest and gave it to Shanba lama to mix with juniper leaves. Shanba lama then placed this mixture on the smoking juniper branches while chanting a special ritual chant to Dzambhala, one of the three main aspects of the god of wealth. The ritual act that gave the god-yak the name Azoma was finished in a matter of minutes, but Shanba lama remained for most of the day, chanting and keeping the smoke offering alight. He did not consume anything apart from milk tea, although his attendant monk ate the fresh *tsampa, chura, go re*, and yogurt that were reverently offered to him. It was during the afternoon tea, after almost four hours of chanting and activity, when I—admittedly aloof from the activities—was made to be a stranger again. The moment occurred when the food was being served.

Shanba lama had stopped chanting and, flanked by Aku Kungo to his left and his attendant monk to his right, sat at the top of the hearth, farthest from the entrance to the tent. Even though he was a highly regarded lama, he was humble and friendly, and their manner with him was, likewise, easygoing and respectful. Daka held out her right hand to take his wooden bowl and fill it with milk tea.

"Oh, Aku, drink tea," she said.

FIGURE 4.2
A god-yak. Photo by author.

"Ya, eat more *tsampa*. Would you like yogurt, too? Have some yogurt," Aku Kungo entreated.

Shanba lama accepted, and he and Aku Kungo talked in low voices about things I did not understand.

By this time, I had seated myself at the bottom of the hearth, at the entrance to the tent, and Pelma Tso was seated close to me, holding my hands and playing with them. Not knowing what to do, and feeling somewhat awkward, I silently observed. Padka was chopping potatoes, bought from Tibetan farmers in a neighboring agricultural village. Panjur had gone to herd the animals back to the spring pastures.

Daka gave me my bowl of tea and said, "Drink tea, Nyima Yangtso." Then to Pelma Tso, she said, "Do you have a bowl? Here, use this, drink tea."

At this time, Aku Kungo addressed Pelma Tso and, with a piece of fried bread in his hand, said, "Ya little girl, give this to the Chinese woman [*gyamo*]."

It was a casual remark, but I was immediately taken aback. And a split second later, after seeing the same expression of shock on Padka's face followed by concealed embarrassment, I felt deeply hurt and angry. Why had he called me that when everyone in the tent knew the enforced emotional and psychological distance that always accompanied the term *gya*? Why had he chosen this moment to alienate me, after I had spent this time with them, trying to be—and becoming—a familiar in the household? As these questions circled in my mind and my indignation grew over this perceived slight, I felt my sense of self shrinking away from the black tent and all its inhabitants. After attempting to brush off the term for a few minutes, I left the tent and sat outside in the warm golden light of the slowly setting sun. I was alone.

But I was not alone for long. After a minute or so, I felt a small hand in mine. Pelma Tso had come out of the tent and, without a word, sensing my hurt, sat beside me. I looked at her and smiled. We sat together in silence, picking up small flowers and arranging them in circles on the ground.

— * —

Before I left Gatsong to stay at Khenpo Dorje Tashi's golden stupa complex in Lhagang, I made a round of visits to the older people who hadn't moved to the summer pastures. In particular, I was keen to visit Ani Palmo. She was the same age as my own mother, born in the year of the Dragon, and was from a neighboring agricultural village. When she married Aku Lungri, who was Aku Kungo's paternal uncle, they settled in Dora Karmo. Ani Palmo had been very friendly to me in my initial months in the community. Walking across the east-west ridges that ran down toward the valley, I tried to keep at a certain elevation so that I would not have to re-climb steep slopes. The location of black tents in the autumn pastures roughly mirrored the location of winter houses in the valley below so that Ani Moko's black tent was now the farthest from Gatsong that it would be. As I approached Taraka, I was amazed by the swift changes to its landscape and the speed of construction for Dorje Tashi's boarding school, marveling at the rows of prefabricated buildings below to my right that had been erected in less than two months. In a week, I would go to stay with Dorje Tashi in his golden stupa complex in Lhagang town, but for now, I continued on my way, over one final large hill, toward Ani Palmo's winter house.

She was, as usual, very glad to see me and caressed my skinny palms with her striking, gnarled hands.

"*Maluh*," she said, using a term of endearment usually reserved for offspring and young children, "ya, sit down, drink tea. What would like to eat? *Tsampa*? Here, eat some *go re*."

She pushed plates of food toward me. "So, how was Ngulathang? Did Daka make you work hard?"

She looked more carefully at my hands and immediately replied to herself, "Not very hard!" She looked at me with faint laughter in her crinkly eyes. She must have been a beautiful young woman, I often thought. Her weather-beaten face was strikingly offset both by her white hair, neatly braided and wrapped around her head in the style of Minyag women, and by her straight white teeth, which she often revealed in a ready smile. The kettle on the yak dung stove started to release a steady line of steam from its spout, and Ani Palmo got up to take a pinch of black tea for the kettle. I looked at her things on the table and caught sight of a photograph, a small frayed photo of her and a man with his face scratched off to erase any active reminder of passed ones. I picked up the photo and looked at it carefully; the man was dressed in modern clothes and looked like a young person. When Ani Palmo returned, I looked at her with a question that faded away as soon as I saw her face. Her smile had disappeared and tears had gathered in her eyes.

"My son," she said, putting the tea in the kettle and wiping her eyes with the back of her hand. "One year ago, he left the house, and he was 'lost.'"

"Huh, you mean he never returned and you don't know what happened?" I asked, trying to understand the exact implications of the word she had used, "lost."

"Ya," she replied. "He left after morning tea to go to Zaka and collect medicinal plants, and he never came home. This was his home," she gestured around us to the space we were in.

"How old was he?" I asked and was surprised to hear that he had been thirty years old.

"And no one ever saw him again either here or in Lhagang?" I continued. "Did you try to look for him?"

"Of course!" she replied. "But the grasslands are very big. After a few days, we stopped. All I could do was to chant *mani* and pray that he would return. But it has been a year, and he is really 'lost.' Sometimes I think that I hear his voice, and I close my eyes and think to myself 'Is it really him?' I listen very hard and I pray, but then the voice goes away. I open my eyes, and there is nothing." She looked at me, clearly and directly, and I felt so sorry.

Still unable to accept her state of unknowing, I persisted: "And he wasn't . . . er . . . killed, was he? In a revenge feud, or someone was angry . . ." I trailed off, seeing the answer in her face.

"Oh no! No, no, it wasn't like that," she said. "It wasn't like that," she repeated.

Then, looking at me trying to understand, she added, "People get 'lost.' This has happened many times before. It happened to Gatsong."

"Gatsong, really? When? Whom?"

Ani Palmo replied, "Many years ago, when Daka and Padka were young. There was another daughter, you know."

"Yes," I said. "I know she lives in Lithang."

"Yes," Ani Palmo replied, counting with her fingers in the Tibetan way, right thumb pressing each segment of her right index finger. "There is the oldest girl in Lithang, then Daka, then there was another girl between Daka and Padka. She was 'lost' when she was around twelve or thirteen years old. I can't remember."

I echoed slowly, "Another girl." I had not known about this other daughter and sister who had disappeared from their lives almost twenty years ago.

"What happened?" I encouraged Ani Palmo to tell me more.

"I don't really know, but one day she went out herding the animals and never came back. They looked all over, and Aku Kungo's wife, she was from Shamalang, you know, and very beautiful, she was so sad. They say that when she died shortly after, it was because of a broken heart. The girl was 'lost,' and they never found her. No one knows what happened." At this point, Ani Palmo broke into a series of chants, "O mani padme hum, o mani pad me hum, o mani padme hum . . ."

She finished by placing her right hand, with her prayer beads wrapped around its palm, in line with her nose in a gesture that denoted an abbreviated prostration.

"For me, my son's loss came at the end of a terrible year. First, my old man passed away. But he was old and had lived a good life. It is easier to understand when old people die, but when young people die . . ." she trailed off. "Then my daughter's husband was killed. They found his body in the grasslands, but no one knew who had killed him or what had happened. We had just done one [death rite] for my old man, and almost immediately, we had to do another. The lamas almost didn't have to leave!" She wiped her eyes again and continued, "And then . . . but we could not do anything because we never found him. There was no body to burn, nothing to do. So I just chant for him and pray that he found his way."

I sat silently, absorbing what she had just told me. Her living room was simple, and through an open door into the only other room, the altar room, I could see photographs of highly revered incarnate lamas. Three prominent frames hung above a row of bronze water bowls. Two butter lamps had been lit, and a vase of plastic flowers had been placed in the middle of the altar place. Unframed photographs of other lamas and incarnates were stuck to the glass and wood cabinet frame that made up the structure of the altar place. I gazed at the framed photograph in the middle and thought of the veneration and adoration nomads feel for lamas and their teachings.

In an environment such as this, the death and loss of relatives and friends were a frequently experienced reality. Furthermore, death and loss did not follow a prescribed succession through generations, with the old passing away before the young. Death and loss occurred without pattern, without reason: parents lost children as often as children lost parents, and grandparents could outlive both children and grandchildren. Moreover, death extended beyond the human; animals could die at any age in any season. There was no certainty in such a risky environment. The harshness of the landscape and frailty of life contributed to the frequency of loss in the grasslands.

For men alone, feuds, and especially the revenge feud, were another contributing factor. Dora Karmo men traveled frequently to Lhagang town, where they and men from surrounding nomadic areas met for trade and socializing. Yet the high levels of interaction in the town offered increased opportunities for misunderstandings: an argument over caterpillar fungus boundaries, accusations of cheating in a sales transaction, even a misinterpreted gaze from another young man could result in a swift jab demonstrating that the long knives carried on the left hips of Khampa men were not merely ornamental. Attempts by local government officials to cull firearms and knives exceeding a certain length had proved somewhat successful, yet the number of killings remained high. Moreover, when such an unfortunate incident occurred and the survivor could be identified, it started a chain of revenge killings committed by the victim's male relatives.

A young man from Dora Karmo, closely related to the household Gat-song, had met this fate. During a trip to Lhagang, he had an argument with another young man from Shamalang. Their argument over the exact boundaries for caterpillar fungus gathering had been simmering for a few days. The young man from Dora Karmo had accused the other man of gathering caterpillar fungus in an area where he was not allowed because it breached the unofficial boundaries set by the village. When the young men saw each other in Lhagang town, the issue was again raised, and their argument escalated into a fight in which the man from Dora Karmo stabbed his opponent. His opponent fell, and without waiting to learn of the outcome, the young man rode his motorcycle back to his family's winter house in Taraka. A crowd of people had witnessed the argument and stabbing. They carried the wounded man back to his family's house, where he soon died.

Retribution was swift. The dead man's relatives immediately set off for the man's house in Dora Karmo, killed him while he was sleeping in the family room, and returned to their own house to burn their dead. This fight would have escalated into a feud and created a cycle of revenge if the village elders had not stepped in to arbitrate and settled the matter. The young men came from communities that were too close; both were from Nanglangma. Neither side took further action. The high occurrences of death and loss are significant reminders that nothing, neither life nor relationships nor resources, can be regarded and treated as permanent. Every person I knew in Dora Karmo had experienced multiple losses of close family members.

I promised Ani Palmo that I would return the next day or the day after. On my walk back to Shehoma, I passed the Taraka area again and observed the activities unfolding below—the construction of Dorje Tashi's school. Unsettled by the growing realization of the impermanence of life in this place, I reassessed not only my own situation but also the physical changes occurring in Taraka, recalling an earlier conversation with Aku Kungo.

We were sitting on the hill called Buri Dong, under a triangle of large prayer flags attached to three-meter-high poles, looking down as the bull-dozer dug up the first chunks of sod in Taraka. I said to Aku Kungo that this was a big change for Dora Karmo. He sat silently for a while and replied that it was but then pointed toward the retreat house of Pelma Kabzung Rinpoche, the head abbot at Derge Dzogchen monastery.

Aku Kungo said, "Over there, next to the cooperative building and school, there used to be five white *chorten*. When I was a young boy, we would play there, and old people would perform circumambulations. Then during the Cultural Revolution, soldiers came. They destroyed the *chorten*, tore them up, and there was nothing." He gestured to the mountains around us and said, "All around here and there, there were forests with many trees. When I was a boy, there were deer and many other animals. Then people came and cut down the trees and killed the animals for furs, skins, and medicine. Now, you see, there are no trees." He looked down at the bulldozer and was silent.

His words made me realize that Taraka had always been a place of change. That Dora Karmo nomads had felt the direct impact of the shifts in lines and landscape brought about by momentous events in Chinese history, such as the Great Leap Forward and the resultant famine, the Cultural Revolution and the public criticisms that occurred. They were still experiencing rapid changes as a consequence of government campaigns. Until this point, I had only distantly appreciated the truth of these transformations. Without experience of the place, and hitherto disconnected from Taraka as a feature in my own memories, I had initially regarded those grasslands as an empty, eternal space in a state of perpetual stasis. But for people here, it had always changed, just as life always changed. The bulldozers and prefabricated buildings were replacing the cooperative and prayer wheel room just as those earlier buildings had replaced *chorten*. Dora Karmo nomads themselves had moved here from another place in Pelyul County. It was said that Taraka had previously been inhabited by individual households of farmers—although what they could have farmed at this altitude remains unclear. In the oral history of this place, a Kagyu sect monastery was believed to have been in the vicinity at some point, and, even further back in its history, it was thought that a Lhasa merchant named Tsongpo Norbu Zangpo had given the place its name. He had been on the road to Lhasa when he stopped beside a hill to drink from the clear streams. He decided to stay there for a few days and called it "Taraka," literally meaning "horse circles," after the legend of Ling Gesar and his horse. In that time, Tsongpo Norbu Zangpo's necklace of *zi* stones broke and scattered on the ground. He was able to retrieve all but one, and it is said that one of these *zi* stones is still buried in the ground somewhere in Taraka.

The continuous changes in place, together with the frequency of death and loss, characterized the impermanence of the world for Dora Karmo nomads. Moreover, everyday practices—living in a movable black tent rather than in a fixed house and changing the name of a child or even of an adult so as to shift the fortune associated with that name—accentuated this impermanence. Such practices emphasized a "light hold" on markers of permanence. All of this was ultimately underscored by the nomads' own understanding of impermanence within the frame of Tibetan Buddhism.

— * —

We traveled by bus and then by car on the northern branch of the Sichuan–Tibet highway, on a road that curved high above the rushing river and wound its way through the forested mountains of Kham. The landscape was initially familiar—I had traveled along the same road in the past. I noted with nostalgia some landmarks I remembered from previous trips when I had worked for Trace Foundation, a New York–based development organization. A lone tree atop a vast mountaintop on the way to the Drango county seat, the last reminder that these mountains had once been covered with a million trees like it. I remembered a Tibetan farmer's house along the road where I had been received by parents grateful for the organization's financial support of their daughter, who was training as a practitioner of traditional Tibetan medicine. A village Tibetan primary school, its outer wall emblazoned with large Chinese characters, had taught children to salute passing cars careening along the bumpy highway road. And, finally, I saw the county seats—towns that housed the power of county governments and a growing number of enterprising Hui and Han shop owners. The modern buildings made of cement with pink tile and ornate metal doors had taken over as the ubiquitous symbol of prosperity and were markedly different from my memory of run-down wood-and-cement buildings. The county seats of my memory had been rather dusty, ramshackle, and sleepy; now they were straight, erect, and bustling, although still dusty.

It was summer 2007. I was traveling with a friend, Palmo*, toward Larung Gar, the immense Buddhist teaching college founded by a renowned incarnate lama of Eastern Tibet named Khenpo Gyurmed Phuntsog. At the junction that indicated the start of a new road, Palmo and I got off the bus and arranged for a small car to take us the rest of the way. It was approaching evening, and we still had a few hours of travel ahead of us. We started asking the drivers of the numerous small cars parked along the roadside if they would take us; many refused because it was late, which meant they could not be guaranteed passengers on their return. Finally, a stocky, curly-haired, sunburned man agreed, but only if we could find two more passengers to fill the seats in the car. In due time, a young monk joined us, but we had to wait for almost an hour before the last passenger was found—an older monk who was to travel half the way. By this time, our driver and car had changed because the original driver no longer felt like making the journey and convinced his friend to take us.

The new driver was young and scrawny, with the jagged haircut typical now of many Tibetan youth, and his car was tiny. Through conversation with the friendly young monk, we were able to acquire detailed information about our destination, including the times of various teachings and the location of the *dursa*, a place for disposal of corpses in traditional sky burials. I was looking forward to the journey, not only for the prospect of witnessing a Tibetan burial practice but also because I was in new territory. No longer tied up in memories, I thirstily absorbed the new sights. The houses were three stories rather than two and unusually top-heavy, so it looked as though the thatched roofs were in danger of toppling over. The road was not as well traveled as the northern branch of the Sichuan–Tibet highway, which lay to the southwest, and the people and animals reflected that in their lazy and relaxed attitude toward the road. We did not arrive at our destination that evening, stopping instead to spend the night at the Serthar county seat, a heavily Tibetan-populated town that was frequently visited by nomads from the surrounding grasslands. At 3,900 meters above sea level, it was one of the highest county seats in Ganzi Prefecture and was located in the border area between the nomads of Kham and the Golog nomads of Amdo.

The following morning, we headed up the mountain with a new driver in a different car. We were approaching the holy and venerated site of one of the largest communities of monks, nuns, and older laypeople in Kham, a community with a leader who had inspired Tibet scholar David Germano to conclude: "Contemporary Tibetans *have* been able to manipulate their Buddhist past in its conflict with modernity so as to be capable of generating innovation and renewal" (1998, 55). This community had grown at such a dizzying rate that the unofficial reckoning of more than ten thousand monks and nuns had sparked fears in the Chinese government of a Falungong-like scenario in its Tibetan borderlands. The clampdown in 2005 had been swift: houses were destroyed and people dispersed. The government imposed a quota on the number of monks and nuns allowed to congregate and placed a related ban on the expansion of buildings beyond fixed boundaries on the mountainside. The sight of the community of simple wood-and-mud residences—nuns living on one mountainside, monks living on the opposite mountainside—was awe-inspiring. My eyes could not find a focus; they switched back and forth haphazardly over the terrain until they settled on a big building, the guest hotel, atop the mountain occupied by nuns. We stayed there.

Because this particular site was highly venerated, as many as twenty corpses were disposed of in one day. On the day of our visit, however, there was only one. We were told that the burial occurs at one o'clock in the afternoon every day throughout the year. Palmo and I had walked from the guest hotel until we found the footpath that hugged the mountainside and curved around to another mountainside path. The day was overcast and the season was still cold, but the grasslands had already lost the brown of winter. Marmots were emerging from hibernation. We walked for close to an hour, and as we approached the site, we noticed the birds: massive vultures that sensed their daily feed was nigh. Some circled overhead; many just perched together on a high vantage point, waiting. We were unsure how close we could approach. Several monks and nuns had made their way to the *dursa*, which was situated in a slightly sunken part of the grasslands. By and large, there were not many observers. Finally, we settled on a nearby slope, sat on the grass to the right of the site, facing the *chorten*, and waited.

I had brought my camera and taken a number of photos of the birds. Despite the colored prayer flags and pieces of bright cloth scattered around, the site felt ominous: a metal fence bordered a small white *chorten* and around it lay a pavement made of large, flat stones. Directly in front of the *chorten* loomed a large rectangle of flattened earth, darkened by blood.

In the distance, two cars approached, followed by a motorcycle bearing the corpse, which was wrapped in white cloth. Given its size, the deceased must be a child. Three men stepped out of the larger four-wheel-drive car and started walking toward the group of observers. As they neared, they veered toward us. They had caught sight of my camera. Their dangling badges revealed that they were Tibetan and government officials from the county seat who had come to oversee the burials. They greeted us pleasantly, sat down beside us, and asked where we were from. We exchanged a few words and asked them a few questions. Eventually, they nodded at my camera and said that no pictures were allowed. This was to show respect to the dead and their families. I immediately conceded, not having thought about the implications of taking photographs, and placed the camera back in my bag. They sat talking among themselves for a few minutes, then said their good-byes and walked back toward their car.

By this time, three monks had positioned themselves in front of the *chorten*, just inside the metal gate. Four family members, including one woman, started to circumambulate the *chorten*. We were at a distance and could not hear the chants of the monks, but one of them carried a ritual bell. The *sha shin pa*, the person appointed to dismember the corpse, was not a family member but one who lived by the *dursa* and dismembered corpses for a small fee. He had placed the body in the middle of the blood-darkened ground, face down and resting on its left cheek so it was turned toward us, arms to the side, and legs straight. He started to unravel the white cloth to reveal the corpse, already gray-white and stark against the bloodstained ground. He walked back toward the monks, who were still chanting. As soon as the *sha shin pa* had exposed the corpse, the vultures started to hop closer, watching, waiting, anticipating. There were between fifty and a hundred birds. More and more had arrived, some circling directly overhead. Most started to lurch higgledy-piggledy down the hill, but they did not approach the corpse.

The *sha shin pa* returned to the body, this time with a sharp knife in his right hand. He stood above it, by the head, and started to decapitate it, cutting from left to right, away from the face. When the head was off, a male family member came to take it away. He walked away from the corpse in a clockwise direction and sat down outside the bottom-left end of the blood-darkened area, farthest from the *chorten*. He proceeded to smash the skull, ripping off the flesh and pulverizing the bones. As he was doing this, the *sha shin pa* started to dismember the corpse, starting with the right lower leg and right hip, then proceeding to the left lower leg and left hip, then moving to cut off the right arm and shoulder, and finally the left arm and shoulder. The torso was left intact. When this work was done, he carried the parts, one by one, to the bottom-right end of the blood-darkened area.

As soon as the *sha shin pa* walked away from the now-dismembered corpse, the vultures that had been hopping increasingly closer and closer started to swoop. A mad rush of birds descended. The parts were devoured in less than a minute. Meanwhile, the male family member had started to burn juniper incense. He had pulverized the skull bones and mixed them into some *tsampa* to feed to the birds. He got up, walked away from the thick smoke of incense, and joined his family, who had been watching the entire time. The monks were still chanting; the ritual bell rang clearly in the cold, thin air. The silent observers slowly got up to leave. Palmo whispered that we should leave, too. After walking back up the mountain for a few minutes, however, I felt compelled to remain at the scene longer. I could not find a coherent, articulate way to respond to the enormity of what I had just witnessed.

It has been written of the sky burial that the gruesomeness of death and the decomposition and disposition of the human corpse all provide a strong teaching on impermanence. The teaching emerges from Tibetan Buddhism and holds important insights into how nomads view the ultimate change in life, namely death, within the framework of reincarnation. Ani Palmo's tears and words showed that she obviously grieved the loss of her husband, her son, and her son-in-law. She felt the losses keenly, yet she also accepted them as part of the impermanence of the world. Her chants for her loved ones were, in part, chants for their journey back into the world in much the same way that an important *terma*, or treasure revelation, when chanted by lamas, helps the dead make their way back to the living.

The *Bardo thodol* (lit., Great liberation by hearing in the intermediate state), usually referred to in English as the *Tibetan Book of the Dead*, is a collection of teachings and meditations that prepare people for liberation through death by encompassing the totality of life and death according to six intermediate stages, or modalities of existence: waking living state, dreaming, meditation, the time of death, the intermediate state, and rebirth. The *Bardo thodol* is delivered close to, at the moment of, or just after death, depending on when the family calls an attending lama to recite the chants. When the text is chanted, there are preliminary procedures, eidetic visualizations, attitudes, gestures and voice tone, and observations of the body and corpse that support the appropriate guidance to liberation (Dorje 2005, 219–24). The attending lama chants passages that instruct the dying on how to understand death-to-rebirth experiences and tells them how to navigate the journey from death, through the intermediate stage, and finally to rebirth. Significantly, the chants are also directed toward the listeners, as a way of helping them resolve their grief in a manner that embodies the ideal of compassion and not sentimentality.

One aspect of the *Bardo thodol*, particularly for those listening to the chants, is tied to the significance of the sky burial:

Are you oblivious to the sufferings of birth, old age, sickness and death?
There is no guarantee that you will survive, even past this very day!
The time has come to develop perseverance in practice.
For, at this singular opportunity, you could attain the everlasting bliss of
nirvana.
So now is not the time to sit idly,
But, starting with death, you should bring your practice to completion!
. . . .
We who are fearless and hard-hearted, despite having seen so many suf-
ferings of birth, old age, sickness and death,
Are wasting our human lives, endowed with freedom and opportunity, on
the paths of distraction.
Grant your blessing, so that we may continuously remember imperma-
nence and death!

— * —

Since we do not recognize that impermanent things are unreliable,
Still, even now, we remain attached, clinging to this cycle of existence.
Wishing for happiness, we pass our human lives in suffering.
Grant your blessing, so that attachment to cyclic existence may be
reversed!
Our impermanent environment will be destroyed by fire and water,
The impermanent sentient being within it will endure the severing of body
and mind.
The seasons of the year: summer, winter, autumn and spring themselves
[exemplify] impermanence.
Grant your blessing, so that disillusionment [from conditioned existence]
may arise from the depths [of our hearts]![1]

1 Dorje 2005, 8–11.

— * —

Padka gave birth to a baby girl in autumn. Daka helped during labor, but it was a quick birth, with labor lasting only a few hours. Padka rested for a day, drinking soup made from boiled yak meat and *tsampa*. She was back on her feet by the following day, although her tasks were more limited than before because she had to breastfeed the child. The baby was very small; she had been born earlier than expected. As was the custom in this area, the baby would not get a name until a year had passed. Then a lama would be called in to perform a blessing, usually in the form of smoke-offerings and ritual chants, and to give the baby a name. This name from a lama was very important because it was thought not only to impart to the child the wisdom of the lama himself but also to protect the child from illness and ill fortune wrought by angry or jealous worldly deities. Until the child received this name, he or she would be called or addressed by a number of affectionate nicknames and terms of endearment: *maluh*, *tsembum*. Occasionally, a nickname would stick and continue to be used even after a lama had given the child a name. The child would then have two names, a childhood nickname and a name given by a lama. And every so often, a name given by a lama would be replaced by another name from another lama. This was done only if the family felt that the child had experienced ill fortune associated with the original name or that the lama who had given the original name was somehow not as close to the family or as highly regarded as another.

Padka and Panjur's little baby girl was sometimes *maluh*, sometimes *zhi mo chung chung*, or "little one [girl]." She did not cry often and slept a lot. Padka's face radiated joy and tenderness as she nursed her child. With the baby's tiny body wrapped in layers of felt and blankets, only her head could be seen as she suckled in her mother's arms.

The baby never received a name from a lama. Less than six months after she was born, she died. It had been a particularly cold winter, I was told, and the baby never made up her strength from being born slightly premature. She caught a cold, and within a week, she passed in the night while sleeping between her parents. I tried to imagine how Padka felt, waking in the morning to find an unmoving baby, perhaps still warm from being wrapped in multiple layers of robes and blankets. Panjur took the baby from the tent to a special place where she was released into a river, attended by the chants of lama Aku Zhiko, who performed the funerary rites and chanted for forty-nine days. Padka grieved for the child and was unable to recount these moments, several months later, without tears in her eyes.

"A nomad's life is hard, Achi Nyima. Life is hard," Padka said. "I felt like my heart had burst. My heart *had* burst. But then I remembered the words of our Guru Rinpoche, and I thought, 'It will be OK. Life is hard, but everything is hard. Everything is impermanent.' Now, it is OK. I still feel sad. Oh, ahah," she half-laughed self-consciously as tears flowed down her cheeks. She closed her eyes for a moment, muttering a chant under her breath. After she opened her eyes and wiped away her tears, she looked at me and whispered, "I have a baby inside me. I hope it will be stronger than the last."

My heart felt deeply for her. "Yes, I am sure it will be. Take care of yourself, eat well, and don't lead out the animals so often. Panjur can do this work," I said.

I recalled Padka's words: "We work, we live, we die. Life is like that." Impermanence. The Tibetan word for this is *mirtagpa*. As teachers at the Sichuan Province Tibetan School explained, *mirtagpa* is the negative connotation (*mi*) of the word *rtagpa*, or a permanent phenomenon that always abides. The opposite of that permanent, abiding essence is impermanence, a concept that is important in Tibetan Buddhist notions of the emptiness of intrinsic nature. Although this term, *mirtagpa*, carries a Buddhist meaning, Padka did not use it philosophically or formally. She used it in an everyday sense to convey uncertainty or lack of clarity, when things or situations were in flux. The only thing one could be sure of was impermanence.

I touched my forehead to hers.

CHAPTER 5

The Lama

Dorje Tashi was born in the grasslands of Taraka in the Tibetan year of the Water Rabbit (1963). His mother, Ani Achung, was from the house named Tralmo and was a distant cousin of Aku Kungo's. Dorje Tashi had only one other full sibling, an older brother named Rangdro. Little is known about his father, although rumors circulated among local people about the identity of this person. When Dorje Tashi was a child, he was recognized as the seventh incarnation of Jalse Rinpoche, whose previous incarnation was known as Pelma Tsewang. He studied initially at the local Sengge monastery before his talents were observed. In 1976, at the age of thirteen, he was sent to Derge Dzogchen monastery, about eight hundred kilometers northwest of Dora Karmo. At Dzogchen, one of the six major seats of the Nyingma sect of Tibetan Buddhism, Dorje Tashi flourished and continued to surpass the expectations of greatness that surrounded him as a child. It was said that he was mentored at the time by Dzogchen monastery's leading elder, Trulku Pelma Kabzung, in the belief that he would eventually lead the monastery. Nevertheless, the intersection of monastic politics and kinship obligations resulted in Pelma Kabzung's nephew being appointed as elder-apparent, which apparently blocked Dorje Tashi's further progression at Dzogchen. Dorje Tashi returned to the Lhagang area to study at the Nyingma Buddhist teaching college established by Khenpo Chudrak in 1985. During this time, he befriended two American research students who would play important roles in his future success: one currently a prominent professor of Tibetan studies and the other a leading development practitioner.

I first met Dorje Tashi in Lhagang at his primary school, which boarded students, mainly orphans from the surrounding area. I was working for Trace Foundation, a New York–based organization that had supported construction of this school. In 2001, Dorje Tashi was already well on his way to fulfilling the expectations of the nomads of his home village, Dora Karmo. Xikang Welfare School, established in 1997, was attracting attention even from eastern cities. Chinese newspapers ran favorable articles on the success of the school, focusing on its charitable works and provision of primary education to orphaned and disadvantaged children. The media also emphasized the school's approach to formal and informal education as a model of Han-Tibetan integration. A standard government curriculum, delivered by Han educators and administrators within a disciplined regime of physical hygiene, morality, and civic ethics to children of Tibetan and other ethnic backgrounds, was a model that the government attempted to implement in its minority regions.

The opinions of Lhagang townfolk were, on the contrary, not unanimously positive. From the beginning, local people had grumbled about the location of the school, situated as it was within a crescent bend of the main river running through the town, saying that this placement cut through the auspiciousness of the river. The large buildings were also, at that time, the first structures encountered on the approach to Lhagang from the highway and blocked the view of the Lhagang monastery behind them. Although unconfirmed, local monastic politics between the leaders of the main Lhagang monastery and Dorje Tashi has played a role in fueling much of the discontent between local townspeople and this incarnate lama. Stories circulated that Dorje Tashi regarded himself as a bird that could simply fly in from his time in Derge Dzogchen and sit atop the local monastic hierarchy; other people believed that his preference for Han people, evidenced by the numbers of Han disciples and employees, disadvantaged local Tibetans. These grumblings were occasionally expressed as extreme views and, importantly, had persisted over the fourteen-year period since I had first visited Lhagang town. I regarded many of these opinions as part of the tensions inherent in situations where personal views clash, especially when an influential other is involved. Despite these clashes, however, local townspeople had benefited in various indirect ways from Dorje Tashi's projects. Increased revenue as a result of the growth in tourism at the golden stupa complex was a major advantage.

And despite these mixed opinions, in 2006, Dorje Tashi himself was asked to take charge of the building and management of a new boarding school for children of nomadic pastoralists in Lhagang township. Before the first shoots of spring appeared in the grasslands, the local education bureau of Dartsedo County called a meeting of the eighteen village heads of Lhagang administrative township to discuss a long-standing issue: how to meet the official policy of providing compulsory nine-year education to children of nomadic communities. Local education bureaus throughout the prefecture were confronting a similar issue. One of them in Drango County had built a boarding school in the county seat a few years earlier as a way of providing formal education to a transient and dispersed population. However, the many problems that emerged from the school had stalled its immediate replication in other counties. The officials told the village leaders that they had to collectively solve the problem of education for nomadic children in such a way as to ensure that local communities supported the solution. The village leaders were also told that a boarding school for nomad children was the proposed way forward and were asked where the school should be built: in Lhagang town or in one of the nomadic encampments of Lhagang township. The village leaders decided that the boarding school should be located in the Taraka grasslands of Dora Karmo. Apparently, they had not wanted their children living in Lhagang town, close to the road and the many vehicles that traveled on the northern road of the Sichuan–Tibet highway. They had wanted their children to live on secure grounds with a big gate so that the children would be safe. Moreover, the person they decided to entrust with this responsibility was Aku Dordra, as Dorje Tashi is known locally.

It is no easy thing, even for a divine incarnate, to persuade Tibetan nomads to give up their pastures. Taraka was the proposed site for the new boarding school, but it was already home to a cooperative building, a school, a prayer wheel building, and the retreat house of Trulku Kaka, as locals affectionately called Pelma Kabzung, a leading Khenpo of Dzogchen monastery, who had lived in meditation in Dora Karmo for more than ten years. In addition, Taraka had eight winter houses, including the house of Dorje Tashi's own family, Tralmo, and the winter grazing pastures of these households. Faced with this complex situation, Dorje Tashi had to negotiate, sending two monks who were his kinsmen but also kinsmen of these families to speak on his behalf. Initially, Dorje Tashi wanted to move five families away from their houses in the immediate area of the proposed school. These were all located beside the river flowing down from Zhamo mountain, the main water source for this area. He offered to pay each household ¥3,000 (US$470 at that time) per pole of their winter houses to resettle in another area of the grasslands. Three households agreed, and one of these relocated to land close to Gatsong, in the shadow of the hill called Pozi Latse. The remaining two households initially refused to move but did move eventually. Dorje Tashi paid these five households compensation for the loss of their winter pastures. In addition, because these households did not immediately give up their herds, they still needed to graze their animals on pastures in the vicinity, which meant that they now encroached on the grazing patterns and pastures of all other households in Dora Karmo. As compensation, Dorje Tashi also paid each household of Dora Karmo for the land in Taraka that he claimed for the boarding school.

But monetary recompense was not the only way Dorje Tashi secured the agreement of his fellow nomads. On May 5, 2006, when I was still living in the winter house of Gatsong, twelve notable incarnate lamas and five hundred monks descended on Dora Karmo to perform a consecration ritual for the school. These lamas and monks were already gathered in the Lhagang area for the first anniversary of the passing of Khenpo Chudrak, a revered incarnate lama who had started the Nyingma teaching college in Lhagang. Many of his students, including Dorje Tashi, had gone on to become influential in their own areas. At Dorje Tashi's request, the incarnate lamas had agreed to come to Dora Karmo to chant for the project and consecrate the ground. It was an unprecedented event for the community.

On the morning of the ceremony, Tsering Panjur was roasting barley outside the winter house. We started the morning milking. The only difference from routine was that Aku Kungo had replaced his usual worn *chuba* with a newer, plum-colored *chuba* and fresh trousers.

"Don't wear that," he told me, pointing to my dirty *chuba*, which I had worn since arriving two months earlier. "We have a *chuba* for you. Daka will help. Also, wash your face," he added. "I am going to Taraka now, and you come later with Daka and Padka. Don't forget your camera!"

After completing the morning work, Daka and Padka both started to get ready: they washed their faces, applied rouge, and pulled out bags of beautiful festive robes. They discussed which belt to wear, which ornaments to put on, and which shoes would complement their outfits. Tibetan festive clothes are a sight to behold: elaborate versions of the daily robe, they are usually made of a dense and handsome wool weave, piped with brocade around the collar and the hems of sleeves and robe. Particularly fancy costumes are hemmed with strips of real leopard—or tiger—skin on the bottom of the dress.

After a while, Daka turned to me and asked, "So, Nyima Yangtso, which robe will you wear?"

Mildly embarrassed, I started to say, "Oh, they are so new and beautiful. Maybe I will wear my own *chuba*. It is fine, isn't it?"

Daka looked at me silently, then turned back to her own toilette, picking out new red wool yarn to thread through her long braids.

Distinctly aware that I had been told by Aku Kungo to wear the fine clothes, and feeling badly that, due to my own self-consciousness, I had probably made her feel uncomfortable, I attempted to right my error. I crossed the room and started to admire the clothes. "Oh, these are beautiful robes. Oh, Padka, that one really suits you!"

Padka smiled. Then I turned to Daka, asking, "Choose one for me, Daka."

She looked around at the clothes that had by now been spread out across the room and started pulling out options. Having chosen one, Daka gave it to me, but Padka said, "It's too short!"

She put it up against up me to confirm that it was. Finally, after several other suggestions, we decided on a deep-red dress with beautiful blue brocade and immensely long sleeves, far longer even than Padka's. As extra-long sleeves are a recent fashion, I guessed that the dress was relatively new and was grateful to them for their generosity.

Tsering Panjur came back into the house. He had not changed out of his red down jacket, grubby from his extended forays to collect caterpillar fungus. As we walked to Taraka, we met friends and relatives from other households making their way by foot and on horse. They had all taken care with their dress. On our way, we cut some branches of juniper to burn as part of the ritual offering.

We approached Taraka, and the dense smoke assaulted my eyes and lungs. Someone gave a shout. In the distance, making their way down the dirt road leading from the mountain pass, rumbled two blue flatbed trucks full of crimson-robed monks standing in the back. As they neared, the nomads started shouting and cheering, and the monks waved and shouted back. This was just the first round of trucks. A small cavalcade of four-wheel-drive vehicles, headed by Dorje Tashi's black four-wheel-drive BMW, preceded the second round of trucks. As the line of cars reached the villagers, all the nomads lined up along the road, took out *khatas* from under their long-sleeved robes, and held them in upturned palms, heads bowed to these human incarnations of the divine. Men had removed their hats, and the long braids of the nomad women from this area, threaded with red and black yarn and normally looped over their heads, hung down their backs. Several nomads had already begun to chant under their breath, their lips moving continuously. One after another, four-wheel-drive cars drove up the small hill to park at the end of the road, in front of the retreat house of Pelma Kabzung Rinpoche. At the end of the cavalcade was a white twelve-seat Iveco van carrying a small group of Chinese people: Dorje Tashi's disciples who contribute generously to his various projects and causes.

As the incarnate lamas emerged from their cars and walked toward the top of the hill where Zhamo mountain looks down on one of its streams, nomads followed at a distance, slowly separating into groups of males and females. Monks put on yellow robes over their deep-crimson ones, and the incarnate lamas stood in attendance, waiting to begin. The nomads, who were by now segregated according to gender, took their places behind the monks, sitting and watching. Several prostrated themselves three times before settling down. Hats remained off, and braids were still down, and the crowd was mainly silent in deference. The overcast day and occasional rain showers provided a counterpoint to the bright clothes of both monks and nomads. The monks chanted for close to half an hour. Their voices carried across the grasslands, past the respectful and silent audience, before dissipating in the wind. Then they got up, gathering their robes around them, and started to mill about, talking quietly among themselves. At this cue, the nomads rose as well.

Dorje Tashi, who had been standing slightly downhill with the other incarnate lamas, started walking down the hill. As he did so, others followed. The crowd immediately parted as he passed, the closest nomads bowing their heads and placing their palms together at the center of their chests. Slowly the entire group of incarnate lamas, monks, nomads, and visitors moved downhill. Dorje Tashi instructed two of his assistants to carry a heavy stone plaque; other monks lugged shovels with a white *khata* tied on the handle. Six nomad men from Dora Karmo were organizing a big heap of white and yellow *khata*, laying them out on outstretched arms, palms facing skyward. When the incarnate lamas stopped, the monks partially surrounded them, to the sides and back, with the nomads across the front. A few of the incarnate lamas were highly esteemed in this area of Kham. Dorje Tashi gestured to his assistants and several shovels were brought forward. He plunged a shovel into the ground in a symbolic gesture of consecration. They passed the shovel around to the rest of the incarnate lamas; an attitude of goodwill prevailed, accompanied by much laughter, as each plunged the shovel into the ground.

The heavy stone plaque was carried forward and placed in the hole in the earth that the lamas had dug. The name of the school, Minyag Dzogchen Primary School, was carved on the stone plaque in both Tibetan and Chinese. The presence of twelve significant incarnate lamas of the area at this event, which Dorje Tashi had organized, further validated the consecration of the school and Dorje Tashi's claims to the site. The location of the school had been a matter of some debate between Dorje Tashi and the leaders of Derge Dzogchen monastery because the land historically belongs to the monastery. Dorje Tashi had chosen the name Minyag Dzogchen both as an acknowledgment to the monastery in Derge and as a way of claiming the land he had secured the right to use, recalling his earlier payments to nomads for the displacement of their animals. Undoubtedly, as well, these discussions were occurring in parallel to the larger geopolitical framing of pastures and the Chinese state. From the state's perspective, these pastures were not "owned" by any of the parties—monastery, lamas, nomads—but rather were the property of the state to which use rights had been assigned and from which benefits could be extracted. The establishment of a boarding school that furthered the state's compulsory nine-year-education policy was, for the present, regarded as one such benefit.

When the stone plaque was laid in the ground, the monks resumed chanting. Again the nomads watched and listened, speaking little among themselves. Finally, on cue from one of Dorje Tashi's assistants, the nomad men who had been sorting the piles of *khata* stepped into the circle, their outstretched arms laden with white and yellow *khata*. The assistant monks gave each monk in the circle a *khata*, starting with the most respected incarnate lamas, apart from Dorje Tashi himself. After every monk had

FIGURE 5.1
Consecrating the ground of Minyag Dzogchen Primary School, Taraka, 2006.
Photo by author.

received a *khata*, the incarnate lamas, still laughing and joking among themselves, walked back uphill toward the large white festival tent that had been erected for them. Everyone followed.

By this time, the atmosphere among the crowd had become relaxed. Men and women were speaking freely, and children were running around. I caught sight of Aku Kungo and made my way toward him. I had been slightly confused about the significance of two consecrations in two different spots and wanted to ask him what was going on.

"Aku Kungo, are you tired?" I asked.

"Not tired, Nyima Yangtso."

"How is it?" I asked.

"Good, good," he replied with a smile. "Then?" he asked, guessing that I had questions.

"Well, what was the ritual down there for?" I asked, pointing to the spot we had just left.

"For the school," he replied. "The school our Tashi Tsomo and Pelma Tso and many other children will go to."

I nodded, "Yes, I see. And what about the ceremony up there?"

He replied, "That, that is for the monastery."

"A monastery?" I echoed. This was the first I had heard of another building for the area. Until then, I was aware only of the boarding school.

"Yes," Aku Kungo replied before adding, "and another building, a big library, which will be here." He gestured to the place we were just walking past, located halfway between the planned monastery and the planned school.

In the next few months, three concurrent building projects would be under way in Taraka. Dorje Tashi thought, planned, and operated on a large scale. The final ritual was the most visually stunning. All the incarnate lamas and monks walked in single file toward the site of the final building project, which would be the largest library in the Minyag area. Dorje Tashi intended it to be a center where visitors, scholars, and interested people would come for information, to study, and to consult original texts. It would be a place of learning and culture. The incarnate lamas and monks chanted and walked in slow deliberation around and across the site, looping around and cutting back, their hands fixed in meditational posture—thumb and forefinger touching—while rotating in circular motions back and forth, right to left. The plans of one influential, visionary incarnate lama would significantly change the lives of all those observing. By enacting his divine purpose, he had managed to ensure the tacit consent of each and every nomad in Dora Karmo.

The day ended, however, in a way that revealed the complex relationship between Dorje Tashi and his kinfolk. When the rituals had concluded, the other incarnate lamas got back into their cars and drove toward Lhagang. Many of the monks stayed behind, although one truck followed the incarnate lamas to Lhagang. The remaining monks decided to play games, racing with one another and kicking a ball back and forth. Nomads looked on and laughed. The formalities were finished, and the atmosphere was palpably more relaxed.

Dorje Tashi returned to the white festival tent and sat on the ground outside. Students from the Xikang Welfare School, around a hundred or so, immediately sat down in a wide circle with him. Tea was served to the students and to Dorje Tashi, along with rice porridge mixed with red dates and peanuts. An afternoon meal had been served earlier to the incarnate lamas and monks, but no one else had eaten the entire day. I was seated with Daka, Padka, and a few other women in small groups clustered around the one wide circle. When the students had finished eating, several monks came out with huge bags of snacks: sunflower seeds, candy, and peanuts. They started distributing these treats to the small groups of local people who were sitting around. Some remained to eat the treats, but nomads were slowly getting up to return home for the evening's work. As I ate the nuts and candy with Daka and Padka, the Chinese disciples of Dorje Tashi came up and sat around him, creating a smaller circle within the larger circle formed by the students. Spatially, these circles doubly separated him from the nomads of his home.

Daka called me to walk home, and as I did so, I passed Dorje Tashi's small circle. He saw me and smiled warmly. I walked into his circle of disciples and approached him.

"So, how are you? You look like a real nomad woman [*drogmo*]," he said. "Is my hometown beautiful?" he added with a grin.

"Yes, beautiful!" I added warmly, glad to have the chance to speak with him even if briefly. "Aku Kungo is very good to me."

"Oh, are you living in Gatsong? So now you are *Gatsong pomo* [a Gatsong girl]," he laughed. "I am glad all is well. When will you come to stay at the golden stupa?"

"After Ngulathang. Is that still OK?" I asked.

"Of course! So, good-bye until then, *Gatsong pomo!*"

He returned to conversation with his Chinese disciples. I walked on to join Daka, Padka, and Tsering Panjur, and we headed home to the evening's duties and work.

Padka asked, "How do you know Aku Dordra?"

"Through my work with the foreign organization, many years ago. I first met him in Lhagang in 2001."

Padka remained silent. Nomads, even those from his hometown, did not have the opportunity to spend time with Dorje Tashi in the same way that his Chinese followers, the students from the Xikang Welfare School, or foreigners such as myself did. Their relationship was simultaneously more intimate and more structured: the former because most knew him as a kin member, recalling the days when he was a child running in their midst, having memories and knowledge of him as one of their own; and the latter because he was their divine incarnate, shaping their social and daily movements and providing the authority to change for all those looking to him for direction and guidance.

— * —

After my weeks at Ngulathang, I left Gatsong and stayed at Dorje Tashi's golden stupa complex in Lhagang for two months (Tan 2010). During this time, Dorje Tashi graciously allowed me to observe him at work as he prepared for the boarding school in Dora Karmo. In return, he asked me to teach him some English and requested that we have lessons every morning when he was free. This arrangement afforded me access to his inner rooms, to meetings that he had with a range of people—disciples, staff, workers, government officials—and to privileged time with him to discuss a variety of issues. Moreover, I was able to travel with him between Lhagang and Dora Karmo as he busily oversaw all aspects of the new boarding school that was to house, in the beginning, six hundred nomad children from the immediate areas surrounding Lhagang.

There was a sense of urgency in the morning air as Dorje Tashi himself inspected half-finished school rooms less than a week before the students were due to arrive. The school's metal buildings were prefabricated and came with a ten-year guarantee. Nonetheless, they were temporary fixtures, constructed to serve the immediate need of housing the children. That year, the school was built as three rows of buildings: the first row, uppermost on the hill, comprised the classrooms; the second row became the dormitories; and the third row was dedicated to the dining room, kitchen, and living quarters for staff. In addition, a tentlike structure with concrete flooring had been built a slight distance away, to serve as the teachers' office and meeting room. Helpers and disciples unloaded supplies and provisions from a big blue truck : metal bunk beds, mattresses, and bedding were piled together in a heap between the third and fourth rows of buildings; desks and chairs were placed to one side, at the bottom of the second row of buildings; massive aluminum pots and pans had already been taken into the kitchen area, along with scores of kettles, bowls, and other utensils. Chinese construction workers navigated around the newly arrived furniture, equipment, and goods. They told Dorje Tashi what they had accomplished as well as some of the problems encountered. Apparently, all the prefabricated buildings were not of equal quality, and there was a problem with the walls on some of the sets. He listened to them and walked on.

When we arrived back at the school buildings, it was time for lunch. We ate rice porridge, although—as usual—a separate box lunch had been specially prepared for Dorje Tashi. While we sat in one of the rooms having lunch, two Chinese disciples knocked on the door and respectfully prostrated themselves before him. He nodded at them and beckoned them to sit down. The man and woman nervously walked in and gave him a report on the electricity situation. One of Dorje Tashi's larger concerns was the provision of electricity to the school in an area that did not have power even though poles and lines, built ten years earlier as part of a government project to carry electricity from Dartsedo to Lhagang, cut across the grasslands. The school was currently running on a generator that provided a limited supply of electricity, but this was an interim measure; a much larger project was under way that would bring power from the golden stupa complex in Lhagang to the school. For this, poles and lines were being erected across the thirty-kilometer distance. The man and woman had come to tell him that a problem with the generator would cut the evening's power supply. This implied that work would have to stop at sunset, which was not good news because everyone was under immense pressure to prepare for registration in less than a week. The main electricity project had also encountered some minor setbacks and would not be ready by the planned date. Dorje Tashi did not react well to this news and spoke some stern words to his disciples, to which they had no reply. They merely sat, heads down, hands on their laps.

Dorje Tashi did not finish his lunch. Instead, he asked his core staff to come for a meeting. Within minutes, those who had been called came into the room, breathless and eager: three Tibetan teachers, a Tibetan helper, a Chinese helper, the former headmaster of Xikang Welfare School, and Dorje Tashi's Lhagang-based secretary Xiao Sun. At Dorje Tashi's request, Xiao Sun started the meeting by giving a detailed report of her work so far. The meeting was conducted in Chinese.

"For living needs, we have purchased mattresses, sheets, blankets, toothbrushes, toothpaste, shampoo, soap, and washcloths. Each student gets one of each, and they are responsible for taking care of their things. For study, we have purchased textbooks and notebooks, as well as pens and other writing implements. For the kitchen, the cooking equipment and utensils have been delivered, but we are waiting for delivery of provisions, such as cooking oil, salt, spices, and also fresh vegetables." The list ran on, and Xiao Sun must have spoken for more than ten minutes. She also gave an overview of the general costs of the items.

As she spoke, the teachers listened and confirmed that some supplies had been received and recorded, while others were missing or had not yet arrived. They also conferred on additional supplies that were needed but had been overlooked. Feeding, clothing, housing, and teaching six hundred children between seven and fourteen years of age was a massive responsibility to shoulder.

Then the head teacher, a local Tibetan woman named Dechen Yangzom, provided an account of their progress in securing Tibetan-speaking mathematics and science teachers for the school. One of Dorje Tashi's topmost concerns was to provide the nomad children with a solid foundation in mathematics and science. However, since the children did not speak any Chinese and it was difficult to find mathematics and science teachers who taught in Tibetan language in Sichuan, he had to look to neighboring Qinghai for appropriate instructors. The Tibetan areas of Qinghai had been subject to different educational policies and had developed a strong curriculum in Tibetan-language mathematics and science at the primary school level. Furthermore, because of the similarities between Amdo dialect and nomad dialect, the transition for both teachers and students was assumed to be relatively easy.

The meeting was interrupted by the unexpected arrival of three officials from the Kangding County Education Bureau, one Chinese and two Tibetan men, who had arrived to check on the progress of the boarding school. The education bureau had committed to paying ¥180 (US$28) per student to offset their annual living costs. It would also pay for the teachers' salaries. With this relatively minor financial contribution, the education bureau not only ensured that it met its nine-year-education target but also benefited from the considerable time, effort, and money that Dorje Tashi brought to the project. This was, in all respects, his project, but the education bureau could point to the school as one of its successes, couched in the language of having brought a government-mandated curriculum to children in a nomadic area. The education bureau thus had everything to gain from this project.

"How are you, how are you?" Dorje Tashi greeted them with a smile.

After formalities, the Han leader spoke.

"How are the interviews for the teachers? We have set the examination in the subjects, and those have been taken."

"Yes, I know. More than one hundred applications from those who were successful in the examination have been received. And we have only forty-seven positions. The interviews will take place in a few days. Dechen Yangzom, do you know her? She is our head teacher, formerly from your Rangaka Middle School, and she will organize the schedule." Dorje Tashi spoke competently, clearly aware of all the details of this large project he was overseeing.

The officials were keen to let Dorje Tashi run the show. The Chinese leader said, "Yes, yes, Dechen Yangzom is a very responsible teacher. She will do a good job with this." He continued, "However, the issues of the mathematics and science teachers . . . you know that we cannot support their salaries because they are from another province."

Dorje Tashi tilted his head in acknowledgment, saying calmly, "Yes, I am able to pay the nine teachers from Qinghai. In fact, it is my *responsibility* to pay those teachers. Don't you worry."

There was a restrained, forced kind of laughter at these words. The leader took out a cigarette, offered it to his Tibetan colleagues, who refused, and lit it in the small room of one of the prefabricated buildings. The seemingly unconscious rudeness of this small act was palpable because smoking and drinking were disrespectful in the presence of an incarnate lama.

He then said, "We are all one family, aren't we?"

Dorje Tashi replied, "Well, you should stay here then! Are you willing to or not?"

Again, the leader forced out a restrained laugh between smoke-yellowed teeth.

Dorje Tashi then continued, "The nomads *wanted* to give me ¥500 per child for living expenses. Do you know why? They told me that even when we give money to the government, our children still don't know how to write their names."

The leader was silent. Then he said in a low voice, with none of the brashness of his former manner, "I am amazed that you got the nomads to give money for the education of their children."

The rest of the brief meeting passed with small talk, mainly among the officials themselves. When the leader finished his cigarette, the officials took their leave.

A few Han disciples, including the former headmaster of Xikang Welfare School, had remained during this meeting. After the officials left, they directed Dorje Tashi's attention to the pressing matter of the construction of one of the buildings. Dorje Tashi walked out into the hot afternoon sun with an orange cap on his head. We sat on the grass overlooking the site, and soon the construction manager, a wiry-looking Sichuan Chinese man, came up. He was smoking a cigarette, which he respectfully put out before sitting on the grass opposite Dorje Tashi in the circle. He looked slightly nervous and eventually said that he wanted to request a favor.

Dorje Tashi looked at him with a direct stare. He said, "Now before you say anything else, I want to ask you a question." Before the man could reply, Dorje Tashi continued, "Do you think that your work has been satisfactory?"

There was a moment's uncomfortable pause before the man answered, "Yes."

Dorje Tashi raised his eyebrows and asked, "Really?"

"*Generally* satisfactory."

"No, I can show you a few problems," said Dorje Tashi. "The walls, for example. They are not straight and have caused many problems for the structure of the buildings."

"But these were problems from the manufacturer."

"I am not interested in discussing where to place blame. What I know is that the problems are there. Now, I ask you again, do you think that your work has been satisfactory?"

The man replied, "There have been a few problems."

"And these problems have occurred more than once. You have not lived up to the contract, and I have to constantly deal with problems in construction and also with the setbacks from these problems. Even the final product is not satisfactory. And now you request a favor. Well, there are still a few days before the school is officially opened, so ask me after you have completed your work, but first, complete your work satisfactorily."

The man bowed his head and left the group. In the meantime, a few other people had gathered around, waiting to ask Dorje Tashi to consider a few special cases. All the past week, he had been entertaining petitions and requests from parents all over the Lhagang area who wanted him to allow their children to attend his school. He had listened carefully to each and told them that he would consider their cases but that there was enough space and funding for only six hundred students. The special cases presented involved some very destitute children. Older nomads came to him, heads bowed, carrying the yellow *khata* reserved for incarnates. They pleaded with him to consider the children. Dorje Tashi called one of his trusted Tibetan aides to verify the information about these special cases, and, upon verification, he immediately agreed that the children could attend the school.

The meeting with his core staff, which had been interrupted in the afternoon, reconvened after dinner. It was 8 p.m., the generator had been repaired, and we were able to turn on the one filament lightbulb at the end of a wire hanging down from the middle of the ceiling. We sat in a circle, all bodies and attention directed toward Dorje Tashi, who was sitting cross-legged on a bed. He asked the main teachers for their thoughts about the school. There was a moment's silence, and then the former headmaster of the Xikang Welfare School, who was also Dorje Tashi's adviser, spoke in response. He talked about Dorje Tashi's dedication to educating children and the successes of the welfare school. These successes were a result of hard work and commitment, such as were needed for the school in Dora Karmo, all the more because everyone in the room had a responsibility to show everyone else what was possible in a nomadic area. They had to make this school not only the best school for nomad children but also the best school for any child. To do this, the children needed love and compassion, but they needed discipline even more.

During his speech, which lasted about half an hour, everyone was silent, expressing neither agreement nor dissent. The Tibetan teachers sat with their heads down and listened. Xiao Sun and the two other helpers also listened. Their bodies remained turned toward Dorje Tashi and not the former headmaster, who was seated a few places away. Dorje Tashi, still cross-legged on the bed, with his wrists resting on his knees and hands palm down, had closed his eyes and appeared to be meditating. When the former headmaster finally finished, there was more silence, and then Dorje Tashi opened his eyes. He looked around the room and spoke.

Anyone who has observed contemporary charismatic speakers before their attentive audiences will understand that it is never the content of what they say that appeals so strongly to their followers but the way they are able to draw people in through their presence: "To the followers, whatever the charismatic leader says is right not because it makes sense or because it coincides with what has always been done but because *the leader says it*" (Lindholm 2003, 2). Words acquire a persuasive power beyond themselves. This is what happened when Dorje Tashi spoke. His posture was straight, although he occasionally rocked back and forth as if he was chanting. He was not chanting Tibetan meditations, however, but speaking in Chinese about his hopes for the unfortunate, the importance of compassion, and the unformed state of childhood. He emitted an unbroken, uninterrupted stream-of-consciousness monologue. At last, he stopped. He opened his eyes and said he was tired. Everyone immediately got up and helped him to the white minivan that would take all of us back to Lhagang. By the time we arrived at the golden stupa, it was midnight.

— * —

On August 26, four months after he agreed to manage the primary education of six hundred nomad children, Dorje Tashi opened his boarding school for registration. The finishing touches to construction were still under way when nomads and children from twenty-two villages in Lhagang and Washul townships traveled to Dora Karmo by horse, van, and foot to register. The nomads had moved back to their autumn pastures, but many still had to travel a fair distance, some for a whole day, to reach Dora Karmo and deliver their children to the incarnate lama. They would have done this for no other person.

Dorje Tashi was inside a white tent on the grasslands. He sat at a central table, and three head teachers sat to his right. Two chairs had been set farther down on the far right edge of the tent for the village leaders. Older children from Dorje Tashi's other school were standing in a wide circle around the front of the tent, acting as a human fence, so that only those who were called could enter. Dorje Tashi seemed relaxed and jovial, revealing nothing of the intense responsibility he had chosen to bear. Soon, two tall nomads walked in, reverently placed two white *khata* in front of him and sat on the chairs on the far edge, holding papers in their hands. They would soon take out more papers from the folds of their heavy and smoke-blackened Tibetan *chuba*, which, in addition to providing warmth, were used for carrying documents and money. The men were the administrative village leaders—Party secretary and village head—of nearby Gutoma. They conferred briefly with the teachers, then the village head rose and called the nomads of Gutoma to sit before Dorje Tashi, facing the tent. As this happened, Dorje Tashi asked for two of the older students from his orphanage, one boy and one girl, to come into the tent and sit cross-legged on either side of his feet. They ran in, reverent and slightly sweaty.

FIGURE 5.2
Registration of students, Taraka, 2006. Photo by author.

The first child's name was called, and a father and son rose to approach the tent in bent stance, each carrying a white *khata*. They placed the scarves respectfully in front of Dorje Tashi and turned to the teachers' table, where the father placed his thumbprint on the agreement. Dorje Tashi greeted the son and told him to settle down next to the older boy sitting by his left foot. The child sat where he was told, his young face revealing a combination of bravado and fear. He was, after all, about to leave his parents for an unknown and possibly different life in Dorje Tashi's boarding school. He looked no more than seven years old. His father came up to give him his small red bag, ruffled his hair, and returned to sit with the other nomads.

And so this continued; one after another, each child was called and placed in a group of five to six children, boys under the care of an older male student from the orphanage, girls under the care of an older girl from the orphanage. Some children clung to their parents, crying that they did not want to go. Most of the six hundred, though, were incredibly stoic: holding back tears, putting up a brave front, waving determinedly to their parents as they were led away from the tent when their group had been formed. Some parents, too, struggled with their tears. Only their absolute trust in this crimson-robed person whom they regarded as a divine being allowed them to willingly give up their flesh and blood for an education they themselves had never received and only vaguely comprehended.

Those tears were not the only ones spilled that day. I left the tent halfway through the afternoon to see where the groups of children had gone. By this time, children from Dora Karmo had already registered, and I was glad to see many whom I knew strutting off bravely out of sight: Pelma Tso, Tsoko, Tashi Tso. For them, the adjustments were less harsh: they knew the place well, and their families would never be too far away. As I scanned the grasslands for familiar faces, I saw Dhundrup Lhamo, Aku Kunchok's six-year-old granddaughter. When I went up to her, I saw that she was crying miserably. I knelt down with concern.

"Dhundrup Lhamo, what's the matter?" I asked. "Are you hurt?" I checked her arms and body. She looked fine but still did not reply. I looked around for members of her family. I couldn't see them, not even Tsoko, her older sister who had just registered.

Then she whispered, "I want to go to school."

I turned back to her, surprised because she was a second daughter and already had her head shaved in preparation for a life in the nunnery. "Do you want to go to this school, like Tsoko?" I asked.

"Yes, but I'm too small."

"Well, you can always go next year," I said, trying to comfort her.

She was still crying, and I was at a loss. Then I saw her grandfather and uncle and gestured them over. Her uncle approached.

I stood up and spoke to him. "She's crying because she wants to go to school but cannot."

He nodded and said, "She's too small." Since I didn't recall seeing her stand against the wooden stick that measured a child's height, I assumed that her grandfather, as village head, had not put down her name for registration.

"But she can go next year," he added, taking her hand and wiping away her tears.

Those who had been chosen would start a different life from what they had known that very day, due in large part to the incarnate lama who was their kinsman.

FIGURE 5.3
Registration tent, Taraka, 2006. Photo by author.

— * —

For the most part, Dorje Tashi was supported by a base of wealthy Chinese disciples who contributed extravagantly to his projects. His charming manner and charismatic qualities ensured their continued loyalty, which some maintained over the course of decades. I met a few of them on a warm summer day when I was at his golden stupa complex. A white tent had been set up at the back of the grounds. He was seated in his usual position at the center of the tent. To his right sat three Chinese women in their mid-fifties who looked quite relaxed with him. He himself was smiling and joking.

"Ah, Nyima Yangtso! Come and sit down," he said when he saw me approach.

The low Tibetan-style tables were covered with plastic-wrapped candies, biscuits, and nuts. Each guest had a paper cup, held in a plastic container, filled with milk tea.

As I sat to his left, facing the other guests, he looked at them and said in Chinese, "She is a research student from Australia, but she was born in Malaysia. Is that right?" He looked at me for verification.

"Yes," I replied. "And now I'm from Dora Karmo," I added jokingly.

"Haha!" he laughed and added, "Yes, now she lives with Tibetan nomads. We are from one hometown."

"Do you speak Tibetan?" one of the women asked me.

"Yes, I do," I replied. "But I'm still learning."

The same one added, "Wah, that's very clever. Is it very hard? We'd like to learn."

I had heard this sentiment expressed before. Wosar, one of Dorje Tashi's resident disciples, had taken to learning the Tibetan alphabet.

"Yes, quite hard to learn well," I replied. "Where are you from?"

The one who had spoken before—she was the most loquacious—replied, "I'm from Shenzhen. And she is, too," she gestured to her left. Then, indicating the woman to her right, "But she's from Guangzhou."

Dorje Tashi added, "They are my close friends."

I smiled and drank the milk tea that had been placed in front of me, wondering if it was these women who had given Dorje Tashi his latest gift, which arrived in the last week of my time with him: a brand-new white Toyota Land Cruiser, with V8 engine, leather interior, power windows, built-in DVD player and screen, and GPS navigation. He had told me that three friends from Guangzhou and Shenzhen had bought him this car. When I asked him how much it cost, amid much clucking admiration, he replied that it was probably more than ¥500,000, but he didn't know for sure.

I had interrupted their conversation, which they continued after these initial greetings were finished.

The woman from Shenzhen said to Dorje Tashi, "I think it is wonderful, this idea to give the Xikang Welfare School students some responsibility for caring for the new students at Dora Karmo."

This is what they had been talking about: Dorje Tashi was toying with the idea of dividing the new students into groups of five, each group with an older student from the welfare school assigned as a mentor and caregiver. It was a good way to manage the new students and introduce them to the general rules of the boarding school and to standard rules of hygiene that they probably did not learn from living in the black tents.

The woman from Shenzhen added, "That's the best way to learn about management! You have to do it!"

She obviously had a long-standing interest in the well-being of the students from the welfare school. The other women were more reticent, although they added their comments and suggestions on Dorje Tashi's ideas for the boarding school in Dora Karmo, particularly for the living conditions and guidelines for the new students.

He listened carefully to their comments. This was a strategy he employed frequently with many different people. I recall when he asked me, as we sat on a hill in Dora Karmo looking down at the school and the students doing their calisthenics, what I thought of a fence around the school and its grounds. His question caught me by surprise. Even though I had known that he planned to build a fence around the land he had purchased for the school, I was not expecting him to seek my opinion.

He looked ahead and drew an imaginary circle with his right hand. "What about a fence made out of white stones?" he asked.

I looked at him and smiled. "Well, there really will be a circle of white stones in Dora Karmo, then!" I was referring to the fact that, in Tibetan, *dora karmo* means "circle of white stones."

He laughed, "Yes, yes, that's my idea!"

I felt, then, quite special that he had thought to ask my advice on something. It made me feel included in his thoughts and plans. Perhaps the three women felt the same way when he talked about his plans with them. It was one of the ways in which his charisma was manifest.

On that day in the white tent with his three Chinese friends, Dorje Tashi suggested that we take a walk around the golden stupa complex after we had drunk tea. A three-meter-high outer wall was being built around the complex. Additionally, the small stupas that served as the present perimeter of the grounds were being painted white. We followed him as he talked to construction workers about their progress. The woman from Guangzhou asked him about this new wall, and he said that he planned to plant grass in the space between the current perimeter and the new wall. She added that it would be nice to have some tables and chairs so that people could sit and read on the grass.

Walking around with Dorje Tashi was always an event. All the people we encountered immediately stopped what they were doing, waiting until he passed before resuming their activities. Hats came off, people bowed. These moments were a reminder that, for those who believed, we were in the presence of a divine being.

When we returned to the tent, an example of this divinity became

FIGURE 5.4
View of Taraka, showing old school, cooperative building and prayer wheel shed (located below the switchback dirt road on Azoma hill), 2006. Photo by author.

FIGURE 5.5
Similar view of Taraka, with old buildings replaced by Dorje Tashi's complex of buildings, and switchback road on Azoma hill now sealed, 2013. Photo by author.

manifest. As soon as he sat down, Dorje Tashi started to talk about three ways of knowing: through the mind or heart, through speech, and through the senses. He gave examples of each of these ways of knowing but said that the highest form of knowing was through your mind or heart. He also said that it was wonderful, even necessary, to know about other things, other languages, other ways of knowing, seeing, and experiencing the world, but most important of all, it was crucial to know one's own mind and follow that path. This path was not necessarily obtained through education, because there were those who were educated but did not know their own path. Rather, the path was acquired through reflection, searching; only by knowing one's mind or spirit would the path become clear. We had been treated, unexpectedly, to a teaching. But this teaching was delivered clearly and deliberately, without the trancelike fervor of the speech he had given in Dora Karmo to his core operations team. Despite my ambivalence toward Buddhist teachings and practices, I was struck by the force, and sense, of his words.

— * —

"Change comes," Dorje Tashi told me in his breakfast room in the golden stupa complex in Lhagang. It was a large room adorned with colors, shapes, patterns, designs, and objects: a frenzy of visual activity vying for sight and attention. Butter lamps and bowls offering water lined one entire wall; the opposite wall was filled, floor to ceiling, with religious books. The floor was covered with plush wall-to-wall carpet in a florid design, and, in the middle, the personal space of Dorje Tashi was surrounded by boxes of Ferrero Rocher candy, sachets of instant coffee, tea from Singapore, and chocolates from Belgium.

"Change comes, and [other] people will come. We need the methods for [dealing with] it; change comes whether you like it or not." He said this as he was recounting how he came to start the boarding school in Dora Karmo and was eventually charged with the responsibility of housing, feeding, clothing, and educating six hundred children.

He told me, "Nomads look and comprehend with their eyes. They say, 'Oh, does this place have enough *tsampa*? What about the quality of the butter?' They look to see these things, and then are happy that if there is enough *tsampa* and butter, their children will be well looked after."

He added, "If the body is comfortable, then the mind/spirit is happy and able to do many things. So I provide these material comforts so that the children will study well."

Dorje Tashi's intimate knowledge of the nomads of his hometown complemented his role as a religious teacher of Tibetan Buddhism and as their authority for change. Nevertheless, this did not imply blind and blanket acceptance on their part. A few local people had expressed concerns over *how* their incarnate lama proceeded with some activities: a felled community willow tree, the growing numbers of Han laborers, workers, and visitors, and worry about how the streams flowing from the ice caps of Zhamo mountain could support the ever-increasing water needs of the ever-growing numbers of residents in Taraka. Yet because Dorje Tashi's two servant monks were from Dora Karmo itself—and moreover, one of them was the son of the village leader—they kept abreast of local discussions and criticisms and conveyed these to Dorje Tashi on a daily basis. He was therefore fully aware of rumblings of dissatisfaction. This knowledge afforded him the opportunity to alleviate many concerns: if parents complained among themselves about their children's diet at school, then Dorje Tashi increased their access to the school and allowed butter, *tsampa*, and *momo* to be delivered to children from home; if there were increased worries about cases of ill health in the school, then Tibetan medical practitioners—a nun and her helpers—were employed to provide teachers and students with packets of Tibetan medicine pills; and if anyone expressed lingering doubts about the loss of symbolic trees and the health of waterways in Taraka, then rituals were performed to increase the fortune of the place.

For this last point, in particular, Dorje Tashi was able to strategize the return of a certain kind of territorial deity, known as *jig ten*. These worldly deities are part of the totality of the world in Tibetan Buddhism, which is composed of the Formless realm (*gzugs med khams*), the Form realm (*gzugs khams*), and the Desire realm ('*dod khams*). The last realm includes the six possible rebirths of worldly gods, demigods, man, animal, departed persons, and hell-beings. Where these worldly gods have been "tamed" into protecting the Buddhist creed, they are regarded as protector deities of a particular place. Because of their immanence, however, they are still subject to feelings of anger and jealousy as well as amity, and often, these deities favor particular humans, who act as their spirit-mediums or ritual practitioners.

More than fifty years ago, Taraka was the home of the Taraka *jig ten*, but this deity left the place after the arrival of the Chinese People's Liberation Army (PLA) and the departure of its own ritual practitioner. The loss of a territorial deity diminishes the fortune and prosperity of a particular place, with a corollary decrease for people and all living beings in the place. Moreover, without its ritual practitioner, there was no way to call back the Taraka *jig ten*. Faced with this dilemma, and eager to restore the good fortune of Taraka, where he now resided, Dorje Tashi creatively maneuvered to invite the spirit-medium of another territorial deity, a more powerful deity known as Zhara *jig ten*, to live in this place. Incidentally, Zhara *jig ten* had its usual home in the snowcapped mountain that bore its name and that dominated the Lhagang landscape. By inviting Lama Sozang to reside in the foothills of the mountains just above Taraka and to perform ritual acts calling on the favor of Zhara *jig ten*, Dorje Tashi fashioned a new, and additional, residence for Zhara *jig ten* in this place, thus conferring this deity's power on Taraka itself. This increase in Taraka's good fortune mitigated the concerns of local nomads regarding other developments unfolding in this place.

Through such attunement to the feelings of Dora Karmo nomads, Dorje Tashi retained their trust, which enabled him to expand the boarding school from 600 students in 2006 to almost 1,400 students in 2013. Parents from as far as away as the Dartsedo county seat were applying to his school for their children. Taraka was expanding in greater ways than ever before because of the vision and labor of one man.

Dorje Tashi told me about his future plans for Dora Karmo on one of my last evenings there in the autumn of 2013. I had spent almost four months in the summer, living alternately in Gatsong household and Dorje Tashi's own golden stupa complex. The evening before I left Taraka, Dorje Tashi invited me to his private living room for the first time during my stay. This was a different living room from the one in his golden stupa complex in Lhagang. He had left that space for his mother and brother and a handful of attendant monks. In this space in Taraka, he had finally combined his living quarters, living quarters for around fifteen resident monks, a large and impressive administrative office, and a prayer hall.

At around ten in the evening, a few of his former students from the Xikang Welfare School, now studying at universities in Chengdu and Gudrah, came to tidy the room and serve us tea. I had taken off my boots and sat cross-legged on a square of carpet opposite him. As a mug of green tea was placed on the low table between us, he offered me various

FIGURE 5.6
View of Taraka from road, 2010. Photo by author.

FIGURE 5.7
View of Taraka from road, showing continuing developments, 2013.
Photo by author.

imported candies and chocolates. One of these included a large block of milk chocolate engraved with the iconic Disneyland castle and beautifully presented in clear plastic wrap. When he offered this to me, I took it and noticed a message in pink fondant icing on the back: "To my father, with all my love." The chocolate had been a gift from one of his Xikang Welfare School students, purchased while she was in the United States taking an intensive English-language program.

"Oh, but I can't eat this!" I told him after translating the words into Tibetan.

He reached out to take back the block of chocolate, looking carefully at the fondant writing. "If you had stayed on to be my English teacher, then I would be able to read this and wouldn't have told you to eat it," he said ruefully, shaking his head. Then, without lifting his head, he raised his eyes to meet mine and a mischievous grin spread across his face.

Dorje Tashi planned to build a new school in Taraka. In 2012, he had practically given the buildings of Xikang Welfare School in Lhagang to the township primary school. This had been a symbolic gesture on his part, a way of removing himself entirely from a town where he had experienced troubled and complicated dealings. In the place of the willow tree so beloved by Dora Karmo nomads, he planned to build a new Xikang Welfare School for orphaned and disadvantaged children. He thought that there was still a need for such a school and saw it as having a different purpose from that of the Minyag Dzogchen School. In the first place, the new Xikang Welfare School would be a smaller primary school. Second, it would focus more on an education that included instruction on how to be a good and moral person. This emphasis was particularly important, and separate from the Minyag Dzogchen School, which, as a school that received government funding for teachers' salaries, had to concentrate more on delivering a standard national curriculum.

For the Minyag Dzogchen School, Dorje Tashi envisioned a high-quality teaching institution that would eventually include a middle-school curriculum. This meant that the Minyag Dzogchen School would deliver six years of primary school education and a further three years of middle school education, which together made up the compulsory nine years of schooling that was one of the government policy targets.

He was fifty now—getting old, he joked—but he had thought of new ways to get his work done: tell other people to do it! The first groups of students from his first class at the original Xikang Welfare School in Lhagang were now attending top universities in Sichuan. In a few years, they would graduate and be competent enough to manage many of his projects, if they chose to do this. And many of them did. They wanted nothing more than to serve Dorje Tashi, whom they dearly loved.

"Eventually, I think I would like a university here," he said to me. "A university that will be the best place in Kham to learn Tibetan language and about Tibetan culture. There is already a library, which will house many great texts and books. It is important to build up to these goals, to make sure that all the right things are in place: teachers, managers, workers. You know the young man Rangshung? His knowledge is very good; he will manage the library. And I hope to get more teachers from Qinghai to live here. Their Tibetan-language level is very high, and they themselves speak a dialect that is easily understood here in this nomadic area, so they feel more at home. The students from the Xikang Welfare School, their Tibetan level is not as high, but their Chinese is excellent, and, I hope, their English will be, too. They have also grown up to be wonderful young people, disciplined and hardworking. And, eventually, when all this construction is finished, I want to make the grounds beautiful, plant trees and flowers . . ."

At this point, he again grinned at me. He was subtly referring to my own subject of research at the time and my attempt to compile a lexicon of vernacular and literary terms related to the natural environment in Dora Karmo. Dorje Tashi knew that the conservation of grasslands—and its grasses, flowers, shrubs, and animals—was always of "particular interest" to foreigners.

We spent the next few hours talking. The conversation flowed from personal stories to my impressions of the first graduates of the Xikang Welfare School. Dorje Tashi's future workforce continued to expand and become even more qualified. I was greatly honored to have this amount of time with this hugely busy person. His vision had already shaped the lives of his fellow kinsmen and community and would continue to do so well into the future.

After midnight, realizing that I had taken much of his time and that I had to leave his complex in Taraka early the next morning, I started to take my leave. For the past half hour, Dorje Tashi had been opening and closing a small red-cloth box. It held a collection of trinkets that he would gather with the fingers of his right hand and let fall, gather and let fall. I could not see clearly, but the trinkets were a combination of coral and turquoise, and a shimmer or two of some metal caught the light. Finally, he let the contents fall again and decisively closed the box.

With his right hand outstretched, he said, "For you, *Gatsong pomo*."

I stuttered, "Uh-uh-oh."

"This is a box of treasure from here, from Dora Karmo. Take it."

I was overwhelmed. Tears welled up in my eyes, and I humbly accepted the box, murmuring, "Thank you, *gen la*."

He smiled warmly, then pulled his mouth into a line as if to reproach me for being overcome by emotion.

CHAPTER 6

Leaving and Arriving

The jagged outline of Zhara mountain was more stark in the summer, when most of its snow and ice had melted. The dark gray slate of its face showed deep crags that were softened by winter snow. But the familiar and impressive sight always made me feel that I had arrived in a place of refuge, a feeling I never had in Chengdu and Dartsedo despite my equal familiarity with them. After leaving Dora Karmo at the end of 2006, I returned in 2007 for more than a month, in 2010 for another month, and in 2013 for four months.

On each return, I stayed a few days in Lhagang town to call on Tashi's parents and catch up with friends. One of these friends is an old woman who ran a guesthouse next to the Lhagang monastery. Ala Soko was a round and smiling old woman in her mid-sixties. She had four children: three daughters who lived in India and a son who was a monk at Lhagang monastery. Her welcoming and warm manner always extended to all visitors and guests, and she had acquired the nickname Amala (Mother) among Tibetans visiting from other areas and foreign guests. Perhaps because there was no older female figure in the Gatsong household, Ala Soko provided a comforting maternal presence during my time in the area, and I eventually came to regard her as Amala as well.

"Ala Soko! Ai, Ala Soko," I cried out as I walked up the narrow wooden ladder leading to her living quarters.

FIGURE 6.1
Zhara mountain, Lhagang, 2007. Photo by author.

"Ai," she responded, "who's there?"

And before I could say anything, perhaps because my heavy boots revealed who I was, she laughed aloud and said, "Yangtso, *maluh*, you've come back!"

I walked into her main room, where she cooked, ate, and slept, and put down my backpack. She laughed happily while I gave her a big hug.

"*Maluh*," she said again, "ya, drink tea."

She turned on the exposed-coil stove and placed an aluminum kettle on the heating element, which grew red as it became hotter. "When did you arrive?" she asked.

"A few hours ago. I went to see Ala Lhamo, but no one was home," I replied, sitting down on the low bench opposite her chair.

Her room, with windows facing the eastern side of Lhagang monastery, was a wonderful place from which to observe the street activity. Often, she would just sit in her chair, looking down at the street, and provide a running commentary on all the townsfolk: "Oh, Lhundrup is back from Chengdu. It looks like he bought a new prayer wheel," or "There's the woman who is a relative of Reshi. Is she visiting again? She must be help-ing Reshi after her husband died," and so on. Occasionally, old friends would sit with her for hours, and they would spend the whole time commenting on what they saw on the street.

I looked at Ala Soko's broad form and exclaimed, "You're looking well!"

"Well enough," she said, smiling, "but my knee is still painful, and I'm too fat!"

"Oh! I brought you some medicine from home," I remembered, taking two large boxes of Panadol Osteo from my backpack and giving them to her.

"Ho ho, thank you!" she said with warm gratitude. "Our medicines aren't good. Most of them are either expired or fake."

"Well, this is from my home, and it is good until 2015. But you can only take two every six hours. Don't eat more than that!"

"Oh ya," she responded, looking carefully at the boxes and then storing them in her locked cabinet.

After hanging her key back around her neck, she said, "Lhamo is in Dartsedo with her granddaughter. But Dorje should have been in the house."

"Well, I shouted and shouted from the street, but no one answered. People must have thought I was crazy," I said.

She laughed again and checked to see if the kettle was boiling. "Then, how is everything at home? How is your mother?" she asked with concern.

She was recalling a previous visit when I told her that my mother had been diagnosed with a severe illness (Parkinson's).

"She's OK, but she has to take her medicine," I answered. "But my father is well," I added.

"Oh, that's good. How old are they?" Ala Soko asked as she did each time I saw her after a long time.

"My mother was born in the year of the Dragon," I replied.

"Hmm . . ." Ala Soko starting counting the animals on her right hand in a standard Tibetan way, using her right thumb to count the "segments" on each finger starting with the right little finger. "She's older than me by six years," she concluded.

Then after a brief pause, she asked, "How long are you in Lhagang this time? Going to Dora Karmo?"

"Yes, tomorrow or the day after tomorrow, I will go to Dora Karmo," I replied. "And this time, I will stay four months."

Her eyes lit up as she said, "Oh! Staying with Ga Kungo?"

I answered that I was planning to and hoped to see her whenever I came to Lhagang.

I stayed with Ala Soko for three nights. In the daytime, I visited other people and caught up with the latest gossip in town. In 2013, caterpillar fungus prices were higher than they had ever been, selling for ¥30 per fungus compared to ¥20 in 2012. But many knew that these prices were still low compared to those in Lithang, where the best fungus sold for ¥100 each and an average fungus sold for ¥80 each. Caterpillar fungus and the money that anyone could make from them were popular topics of conversation.

Many Lhagang townsfolk also told me to expect big changes in Dora Karmo. Since my last visit in 2010, new houses had been built with financial help obtained through the government's Nomad Settlement policy. Construction of new houses in one administrative part of Dora Karmo had started in 2011 and was completed in 2012. The township government had contributed ¥30,000 per house, and nomads who could afford it put in ¥20,000. However, the houses were built by Chinese contractors and were in a "Chinese style." In another administrative part of Dora Karmo, the government contributed ¥25,000, but nomads built their own houses in traditional style. Nomads could add to, or subtract from, this amount as they wished, and construction was still ongoing.

Lhagang monastery had started to build its own Buddhist college on Jambayang hill, just as the Nyingma Buddhist teaching college was expanding its own buildings and enrollment. But the topic on everyone's lips was the sale of Dorje Tashi's Xikang Welfare School to the township government in 2012. With more than 1,000 students at his boarding school in Dora Karmo, Dorje Tashi decided to focus all his attention there. He had apparently sold the buildings of Xikang Welfare School to the Lhagang Primary School for an undisclosed sum. Most townsfolk thought that he had sold the school for a song and regarded it as his conciliatory parting gift to the town in view of their difficult relationship. I had found it discomfiting at times to negotiate the tension resulting from my respect for Dorje Tashi and the contrary opinions of others with whom I was close. I partly reconciled this conflict by telling myself that someone with a vision far larger than that of anyone else in the immediate area would logically come up against people with ideas that were provincial and somewhat closed. But this was never a fully satisfying explanation for me, and I was always glad that I could maintain some distance form the situation due to my frequent comings and goings.

— * —

The bumpy dirt road from Lhagang to Dora Karmo had been replaced by a smooth sealed road. It was part of a new thoroughfare that ran from Dartsedo to the new airport, bypassing Rangaka, and channeled visitors to Ganzi Prefecture directly to the northern branch of the Sichuan–Tibet highway. The journey from Lhagang to Dora Karmo now took about twenty minutes, in contrast to the forty-minute car ride and two-hour horseback ride of the past. As the little hired van drove past newly constructed Tibetan-style houses in the village of Shamalang and a "new model village," I silently marveled at the changes. Only the topography remained comfortingly familiar, the ever-looming form of Zhamo mountain and the wide expanse of Gani Rika valley, as the van climbed higher, toward Azoma pass, which the household Gatsong crossed on its way to its summer pasture, and the gradual descent along hairpin turns that took us past Azoma hill toward Taraka. The numerous hills along this wide valley—Jatango, Buri Dong, Rimtoma, Gehalib, Gawu Jabtri, Zhaseb, Galuma, Shango Tongchu—enveloped me. At the same time, the imposing structure of Dorje Tashi's new complex was impossible to miss. A massive, six-story, concrete block, the Minyag Dzogchen Primary School, was flanked on one side by an equally large golden-roofed cultural center. The old cooperative building, school, and prayer wheel room were gone. Above both the school and the cultural center was a smaller complex of three buildings: two peach-colored concrete buildings that housed his staff and a growing base of visitors and disciples and one central multi-purpose building that contained a prayer hall, a kitchen and dining area, living quarters for his monks, an operations office for his projects, and a meditation room. In this central building, at the highest point of the combined complexes, were Dorje Tashi's own rooms, which only a select few could enter.

The van driver dropped me off on the side of the main road. The landscape of Taraka had been completely transformed even beyond Dorje Tashi's complex. Rows and rows of white concrete houses flanked both sides of a paved road that ran from the main road to the large red gate of the complex. Small shops selling sundry mass-produced Chinese items— soy sauce and packets of instant noodles—dotted both the main and the side roads. That feeling of enveloping embrace from the surrounding hills

FIGURE 6.2
View of Dorje Tashi's complex, Dora Karmo, 2011. From left: Minyag Dzogchen Primary School, administrative and residence buildings, Minyag Cultural Centre. Photograph by Nicola Schneider.

vanished in this assault of silent concrete and plastic. Taraka, once a fertile grassland valley, had become a little town.

I suddenly felt as unfamiliar as I had been when I first arrived in Dora Karmo seven years before. With the same pack on my back, the long uphill walk to Dorje Tashi's red gate was as strenuous as the walk to Gatsong seven years before. The gate was locked when I arrived; there was no one around. I tried to call Dorje Tashi on his mobile phone, but it was turned off. I decided to walk around some of the new houses just outside the red gate, wondering if I would meet anyone I knew. The whole place was quiet apart from a few cowering mongrels, the kind found in towns rather than in a nomadic area.

As I wandered away from the concrete road and toward patches of grass amid the construction rubble from the new houses, I noticed two figures sitting on a slope about fifty meters away. One of them raised his hand, and I soon realized who it was. He was sitting perhaps in the same spot where I had first met him seven years before. With a burst of gladness in my heart and with old hurts never openly resolved but nonetheless well forgotten, I rushed up as quickly as I could with the heavy pack on my back. When I reached him, I sat by his feet and grabbed his brown and callused hands in mine.

"Aku Kungo!" I cried, looking up at him.

His eyes disappeared into laugh lines, and his whole face beamed. "Ya!" was all he said.

We sat silently for a few seconds, each assessing the three years that had passed since our last meeting in 2010. His hair was grayer and his face more wrinkled, but he looked the same otherwise.

"Ya," he said again, still smiling broadly.

"Did you know I was coming?" I asked, adding, "I tried to call Panjur's mobile phone, but it was turned off."

He replied, "I heard you were in Lhagang, Tashi saw you. I was here [in Taraka] yesterday, thinking you might arrive."

My heart filled with happiness. I was at a loss for words and looked at the youth sitting beside him, who was watching us closely.

"Ya, let's go to the house," Aku Kungo said, trying to rise.

"Oh, first I have to see Aku Dordra. He is expecting me." I gestured in the direction of the complex.

Aku Kungo attempted to rise again, this time getting to his feet with a loud *mani* chant that seemed to give him a needed burst of energy.

"Oh ya, come to the house after you have talked with Aku Dordra," Aku Kungo said and slowly limped down the slope to the concrete road. "Make sure you come, Nyima Yangtso!" he emphasized while slowly walking away.

Taraka had changed beyond recognition, but as I walked north along the same path I had first taken with Aku Kungo seven years ago, the land and people once again became familiar. Ani Moko and a few others on horseback, on their way back from collecting caterpillar fungus on Zaka Megyal hill, greeted me happily as I passed her winter house. After conversing with them for a few minutes, and promising that I would visit either tomorrow or the day after, I continued along the path. A new Tibetan-style winter house had been built beyond the little stream that rounded toward the Dora Karmo River and Aku Kunchok's winter house in the distance. The familiar bump of Pozi Latse hill, with another new Tibetan-style winter house at its base, signaled my approach to Gatsong. An unfamiliar sound made me look up: an airplane was flying just overhead, on its way to the new Kangding airport less than thirty kilometers away. I stared at it for a while and then made my way across the rocks and shrubs toward the main gate of the house. Well aware that the household would have new dogs that would not know me, I picked up a few stones and put them in my jacket pocket.

"Aku Kungo," I called out and did not have to call again because I spotted him in the distance, behind the house, within a fenced area that was new to me.

I walked quickly toward him and offered him a *khata* and a large bag of green apples.

"Oh," he said, happily receiving the mark of respect and gift of goodwill.

We turned toward the renovated house. A second story had been built since my last visit so that the ground floor where they used to live now sheltered Panjur's motorcycle, provided storage space for dried yak dung, and housed the occasional small yak calf. A woman came out of the house to tie up the dogs. It was Daka.

She came toward me, and a smile lit her face when I took her hands.

"Nyima Yangtso," she said in her low voice. "You've come back."

"Are you well, Daka?" I asked her.

"Yes," she said. "Come in the house," she added, gesturing.

"What are the dogs' names?" I asked as we walked toward the house, knowing that the old dog that had snored in my ear in the black tent all those years ago had died.

"This one is Samgo." She pointed to the large older dog, tied up inside the front fenced area and barking ferociously at me.

"And the other?" I asked of the younger dog tied up outside the fenced area, just beyond the front gate, and barking just as ferociously.

"He doesn't have a name yet," she replied. "Panjur just got him."

We walked inside, and I found that the ground floor was now a single open space. I tried to imagine the old room where I had first stayed with this same family almost exactly seven years ago. It did not seem possible, because the actual space seemed much smaller than the space I remembered. I waited for Aku Kungo to go up the stairs first; its steps were so narrow that it was more like a ladder. I then followed him to this new part of the house.

"When was this built?" I asked as we were climbing.

"Last year," he replied and then grunted a loud "umph" at the effort when he reached the top. He opened the door to the sounds of children's voices.

When I walked through the door, I was greeted by four pairs of eyes staring curiously at me. Tsetruk Dorje was six years old. I had met him three years earlier during my last stay at Gatsong. At that time, Sonam Garjud was less than six months old, and here she was, a three-year-old girl with pigtails and a mischievous grin. In the corner of the room, two new pair of eyes looked up at the unfamiliar person in the doorway. Kabzung Tsomo was barely eighteen months old and just learning to toddle unsteadily. She was slightly cross-eyed. Her sister was wrapped in robes and blankets and looked remarkably similar to Padka's first baby. She was six months old and did not yet have a name. I sat down on the floor, close to the two younger children.

"What's her name?" I gestured toward Kabtso. Aku Kungo replied, and I called to her, urging her to come to me with my open palms. She smiled and laughed, clapping her hands, but remained seated.

"Where are Padka and Panjur?" I asked.

"Gone caterpillar [fungus] collecting," Daka replied.

"Oh yes, I heard the prices are very high this year. Is that right, Aku Kungo?" I said.

"Yes," he replied. "And we don't know why. But it is good for us," he added, turning on the television.

The television! The prefectural government had connected the entire area to electricity in 2010. Now the family had a television and a satellite dish on the roof of the house. Mobile phone reception was also available across the entire area, including Ngulathang. I looked at the television and took in the new surroundings. The new room was the same size as the old room I had first stayed in, but now there was a whole other room on this second floor, separated by a door frame and a door curtain. This was Aku Kungo's room, which also served as the altar room and storage room for sacks of *tsampa*. Their living space had doubled along with the number of persons in the household.

"Ya, Nyima Yangtso, drink tea," Daka said, after the water had boiled and she had prepared a fresh kettle. "Your bowl?" She held out her right hand, so familiar, for my beloved wooden bowl.

"Oh, it's broken!" I said, still sorry about it. "After I left you in 2010, I packed it in my bag. And it got broken in the airplane. I have no bowl now, but I brought you some new bowls. Here." I reached into my backpack and took out four new bowls purchased from the Carrefour supermarket in Chengdu.

"Ya," Daka said, reaching out for the bowls and putting one aside for me. Then suddenly, "Hai! Sonam Garjud, what are you do-*ing*?!"

I turned to see the impish face looking up at me with a big grin. She had reached into one of my jacket pockets.

"Haaaaaa!" she cried, getting up and running quickly around the room. She didn't speak well for a three-year-old, but she climbed and ran really well.

"Huuup!" Tsetruk Dorje grabbed her to stop her from running in circles. He pushed her aside and started cycling his little plastic tricycle in circles around the little room.

The room suddenly erupted into a cacophony of sounds and cries. Sonam Garjud, chastened at being treated so, stamped her foot and started to chase Tsetruk Dorje, intent on hitting him with her little fist. He faked an expression of fear, pedaling furiously to get away from his angry little sister. The chase soon turned to fun. Kabzung Tsomo chuckled with delight, struggling to get to her feet to join in. And the baby girl quietly observed with her large, unblinking eyes.

Footsteps thudded on the wooden stairs, and the door opened. It was Padka. When she saw me, she smiled broadly, and her eyes crinkled into crescents.

"*Khaliy, khaliy, khaliy, khaliy!*" she said loudly.

Sonam Garjud ran to hug her knees.

Padka said, "Ya! Drink tea, Achi Nyima. Are you tired?"

I replied with gladness, "Not tired, Padka. Are you tired? Got many caterpillars?"

She smiled in her special way, not wanting to seem too pleased with her harvest. "Good," she replied with a small nod of her head.

"*Khaliy, khaliy, khaliy, khaliy!*" Panjur's voice boomed as he entered the room. We went through the same formalities. The entire household was now together, and I felt incredibly happy. They looked the same, they were well, and there were now four children in the home. It was noisy and full of life.

I showed them photos of my family and my life in Australia, which they were happy to see.

"No children, Nyima Yangtso?" Daka asked with a lopsided grin. "What about a husband?"

"No, no children, but here's my husband," I pointed to one photo.

Padka smiled. "Where is your friend, Perlo?" she asked, remembering the time when Perlo had visited the household while I was doing fieldwork to talk about his plans to start his own nonprofit organization called Rabsal.

"He's home in Dzachukha with his wife," I replied. "Tomorrow or the next day, I want to show you his film, *Summer Pasture*. It is about nomads' life in Dzachukha."

Panjur asked, "Did he really make a film? How?"

I replied that Perlo had made a film with the help of two really good American filmmakers.

I couldn't wait to show it to them and to see their reactions. While we were talking, the children had taken to sitting beside, or in the lap of, their favorite adult: Tsetruk Dorje beside Daka, Sonam Garjud next to Padka, and Kabzung Tsomo in Panjur's lap. Aku Kungo sat on the only chair in the room and switched his attention between the television and our conversation.

"Oh, it's getting late. Daka, it's getting late. What should we eat for dinner? Achi Nyima, what do you want for dinner? *Tsampa*? Rice?" Padka asked.

"*Tsampa* is good, rice is good, anything is good," I replied.

As we were discussing and I got up to help, there was suddenly a loud thud and a wail. Sonam Garjud was sitting on the floor, crying wholeheartedly. Tsetruk Dorje tried to look innocent; Garjud was incoherent with sobs.

"*Tse*-truk *Dor*-je!" Padka shouted, going up to him to cuff his head and twist his ear. "What did you do!"

"Aaaiiii!" cried the boy, running behind Daka to protect himself from his mother's wrath. No one had seen anything because Aku Kungo had left the room and Panjur had been busy attending to Kabzung Tsomo.

"You naughty boy! I'm going to get you later!" Padka shouted at the cowering boy, but a sideways glance at me revealed her twinkling eyes.

She covered her head with a scarf and went outside to herd the animals.

Dinner that evening and for many of the evenings afterward was completely without meat. This was a marked difference from even three years ago, but certainly from 2006, when we ate either pork or yak meat daily. Some time later, Panjur almost apologized for this lack of meat, asking me if it was not too difficult to eat "leaves" all the time. He was referring to the vegetables, a sort of brassica, that they had planted even within the front enclosure of their winter house. I said that it was and asked him how he felt about it. He screwed up his face in reply. "Leaves" were not tasty. The reason behind their mainly vegetarian diet was Tsetruk Dorje. More than two years ago, Aku Kungo had taken the boy to meet Dorje Tashi. The meeting was an opportunity for Dorje Tashi to speak with the boy and to decide his future path: whether he would enroll in the boarding school or go to the local Sengge monastery when he was old enough. Nothing was decided at that meeting, but Dorje Tashi's advice was for the boy to not eat meat. And because it was nearly impossible to keep him from eating meat while the rest of the household did, Aku Kungo thought it would be best if everyone stopped, at least when Tsetruk Dorje was present. Panjur said that he still ate meat when he went to Lhagang, and that the other household members ate meat on the rare occasions when Tsetruk Dorje was away, for example, at the house of his paternal grandfather, Thubten.

Conversations with Panjur revealed how aspects of their lives had changed. Large tracts of grasslands in Taraka were no longer available or usable for grazing, and therefore the overall land in the winter pastures of Dora Karmo had decreased quite significantly. To make up for this, several households, such as Jonla and Gatsong, grazed an increasing number of their animals in a different winter pasture. Gatsong now grazed more than half its herd in Karchag, the forest where Padka and I had an earlier scare with possible wolves, during the winter. During the winter, Daka left the household, staying in a simple shack on the eastern edge of the forest and taking care of the animals. Panjur said that the household Jonla increasingly used the pastures beside Zaka for their animals. Of greater interest to me, however, was a subtler parallel practice. In order to supplement the animals' feed in the winter, the household had started to sow grass seeds around the winter house and to make hay. Panjur said that this was hard work and jokingly added that they were becoming more and more like farmers. In essence, though, they continued to live a nomadic life that was still primarily dependent on the dairy production of their animals for sustenance.

— * —

In 2013, Dorje Tashi's boarding school had 1,400 students and was growing. Children now came from not only nomadic areas but also farming communities. The school's reputation had spread far, and some households in Dartsedo, the prefectural seat, had petitioned to place their children here. The school building itself was fully ensconced within the high white wall that Dorje Tashi had built: his own version of "the circle of white stones."

Once a month during the school year, families could enter through the big red gates and spend the day with their children. Fathers sat in classrooms next to their sons and daughters while the teachers taught lessons. Mothers, grandmothers, and aunts prepared picnics on the grounds, laying out a feast of *momo* and *go re*, plastic-wrapped sweets and biscuits, and condensing a month's worth of love and preparation into a single meal. The entire place was overrun with minivans, motorcycles, cars, and people. Construction work stopped for the day.

During one of these open days, the Gatsong household—with the exception of Padka, Kabzung Tsomo, and the baby girl—went to the school. Tsetruk Dorje, particularly, was excited to see his two *achi*, or older sisters. This is what he called the teenage daughters of Padka's and Daka's older sister who lived in Lithang. On that morning, the whole community was on the move toward Taraka. Women walked on the path, carrying bags of food and bottled drinks. Men rode on motorcycles, shuttling back and forth taking the elderly or young to Taraka. It was a festival as large as the summer horse race. Daka had made plenty of vegetable *momo* and *go re*. In addition, she had bought packets of instant noodles, biscuits, sweets, bottles of soft drinks, and bubble tea from Lhagang town during our last trip there. This had been just a few days ago, when the three of us—Panjur, Daka, and I—went to sell yak meat from a two-year-old animal that had broken its leg and died. We piled onto the motorcycle together with a fifty-*jin* carcass that Panjur had butchered for the twenty-minute ride into town.

We spread out this picnic under the area's sole willow tree. Construction sheds and vehicles surrounded the place. Ani Tseko, who was Aku Kunchok's wife, entreated me to eat some of her meat *momo*. She was happy that I would get to see her granddaughters, Tsoko and Dhundrup Lhamo, saying that they had grown big and that I should speak English with Tsoko, who was a top student in the school. I was eager to meet the girls who, seven years earlier, had been my companions—talking and playing with me when the adults were busy. I was especially keen to see Pema Tso. People got up and walked around, then sat down and ate a little. Everyone milled about, anticipating the arrival of the children. There was palpable excitement in the air.

When the bell rang and the children finally emerged, a cacophony of sounds erupted—high-pitched greetings and cries from the younger ones, calls and conversations with the older children. It started to drizzle. I sat under the tree, absorbing the energy around me and eagerly awaiting the arrival of the girls. Tsoko ran up first; she greeted her grandparents, her father, and her uncle and sat down, exhaling loudly. When she was finally settled and looked around, she caught my eye, and her eyes grew round. Not knowing what to say, she looked at her uncle and grandmother.

"Ya, say hello. Don't you remember?" her uncle urged.

While I had invariably seen many of the adults in the community on my return visits over the past seven years, I had not seen any of the girls since my departure at the end of 2006. Tsoko was tall and slender, with an open face and intelligent eyes. She shyly looked down and then smiled broadly at me.

"Are you tired?" I asked her.

"Not tired," she replied. Her grandmother gave her a *momo*.

"What class did you just have?" I asked.

"English," she replied.

"Ah!" I said, now aware that everyone was listening to us. I started to speak with Tsoko in English and was impressed by her ability. Her pronunciation revealed that she had an English teacher who had trained in the Chinese system, but otherwise, she was able to carry on a simple conversation. With each word, she got over her initial shyness, and, by the end, we were chatting nicely about her classes and her friends.

In the middle of this conversation, Dhundrup Lhamo, her younger sister, arrived. Already intensely shy as a six-year-old, she was even more so at thirteen. She immediately recognized me and immediately looked away with a red face, burying her head in the crook of her uncle's elbow. Urging and encouragement from her family to speak with me did not help, and she finally went away with her uncle to walk around the school grounds. I did not manage to speak with her during the few hours we all spent together.

"Where is Pelma Tso?" I asked Wonam Drolma. Wonam Drolma had graduated from the school just two years ago but had not pursued further education. She was particularly adept at harvesting caterpillar fungus and, furthermore, had not shown much interest in her studies.

"I don't know. Father went to her class, so maybe they are still there," she replied.

After another half an hour or so, Pelma Tso arrived. She had grown into a sturdy woman, sturdier than Tsoko, and she now wore glasses, but the same sweet smile lit up her face when she saw me. Because I sat under the tree, surrounded by Daka and the children, I was unable to speak with her directly. She sat almost opposite me in the large circle of people. Her father and mother plied her with food and asked her many questions. She answered quietly and looked at me a few times. The rain got heavier. Umbrellas opened, and Tsoko's father, Woje Tashi, quickly set up a Western-style tent, bought in Lhagang, that could seat five children and two adults. I went in with Sonam Tsanyi, Tsoko's monk uncle, and five other children. Pelma Tso went with her parents into their own modern tent.

It was only later in the day that I managed to speak a little more with Pelma Tso. The quiet and kind girl had grown into a quiet and kind teenager. She liked her classes and enjoyed studying. She would likely follow in the footsteps of her oldest sister, Pelma Lhaka, and continue her studies in the Tibetan middle school in Rangaka. She asked me about my life in Australia and was happy to hear about the little that I could share. Ani Chonyi Wangmo frequently interrupted the conversation, though, entreating her to eat. Even after all these years, Dora Karmo parents worried about whether their children were getting enough to eat at the boarding school. Pelma Tso had to leave after just three hours. The next time her family would see her would be for a brief three weeks in Ngulathang when the school had its summer vacation. We said good-bye, and I said I was looking forward to seeing her again in Ngulathang. She smiled in reply. She didn't realize, after all this time, that I still remembered the compassion she had shown me one day when she was just nine years old.

— * —

We set up the black tent at almost exactly the same spot in Ngulathang that we had used even years ago. There had been a bit of doubt and worry that the household, like a few others, might not have moved to the summer pastures. That year, the animals had contracted an illness called *katsa* (literally, "hot mouth"). Their mouths became swollen, their eyes gummy with thick yellow fluid, and their hooves eventually became swollen, too. A number of animals from several different herds had already died. With this illness, also known as foot-and-mouth disease, the animals were too weak to walk the whole way from the valley to Ngulathang. Several households, such as Jonla, went to nearer pastures. Aku Kungo in particular was concerned that the household's larger animals might contract the disease and not be able to carry the heavy loads all the way. For a full two weeks before we were supposed to leave, everyone watched those animals closely.

On the day of the move, we left on horseback. Only Aku Kungo remained behind in the winter house. He told me to go slowly and to stay with Daka. After half an hour, it became apparent that the herd was splitting up: the healthy animals walked briskly and without any problem, but a number of other animals, including a few baby yaks, were having difficulty. They stopped often, panted heavily, and coughed frequently. Panjur decided that he would proceed on horseback with the healthy animals; Padka followed him with the children on the other horses. Daka and I were to walk slowly behind the ill animals and take our time. It took us nearly ten hours to arrive in Ngulathang. One of the baby yaks was unable to walk, and Daka had to carry it on her back more than half the way. A yak piggyback. In addition, we had to herd the remaining fifteen or so animals, which were scattering and wandering into other herds that were also on the move. When we finally joined the rest of the household, they had set up a white canvas tent, a *gur*, for the night. Both Daka and I were glad to sit down and drink tea. We had not eaten since dawn.

Our neighbors were the same, except that Chomo now lived with Ani Moko in the same black tent. Her husband had died a few years ago, the tragic result of an ongoing revenge feud. As long as a nomad man had "enemies," he was never fully safe. Ani Moko was the same as ever, with a few more gray hairs around her temples. She dropped in as often as she had always done and brought with her as much jollity as I remembered. One day, when she came in for some tea and gossip, Tsetruk Dorje had decided to suckle on his aunt's breast. This was something he did occasionally, particularly when he was feeling sleepy or unwell.

"Piiiii! Tsetruk Dorje! Aren't you ashamed? A big boy like you looking for a breast? How old are you? Six years old?! Piiiii!"

He looked at her and flashed a grin. He didn't move. Daka smiled self-consciously and tried to push him away.

When he still didn't move, Ani Moko suddenly grabbed his leg and said, "Here! You want a breast? I have a big breast for you!" while lifting up her shirt to reveal an ample bosom.

"Aaaahhh!" cried Tsetruk Dorje, trying to free himself amid loud guffaws from Ani Moko and Daka.

"Come on, come here! Here's a big breast for you!" Ani Moko continued, laughing until tears ran down her face.

Sonam Garjud, initially shocked by what was happening, soon joined in the fun and tried to push Tsetruk Dorje toward his maternal grandaunt. As was usually the case when these two older children played, the fun soon gave way to tears. Garjud ran out of the tent, crying and looking for her mother.

Padka adopted a certain attitude toward her four children. She tended to give the younger ones the benefit of the doubt, and because she was hardly around to observe their interactions, she was continually whacking Tsetruk Dorje—favored by both his grandfather and Daka—for his misdemeanors. She was obviously the disciplinarian of the household and the one person whom Tsetruk Dorje feared.

Panjur and Daka would always say to him, "Wait until your mother gets back!" or "If you don't behave, we'll tell your mother!"

But she was also extremely gentle with him when he behaved well. Perhaps realizing that he would soon leave the household, either for Dorje Tashi's school or for Sengge monastery, she often sat with him in the black tent and told him old children's tales, which he particularly loved to hear. Padka said to me, "He loves those stories, and when he leaves us, he won't hear them anymore. So I try to tell him as many as I can."

In contrast, Sonam Garjud was not interested in sitting around and listening to stories. She was an active little girl and loved to help her mother collect kindling or carry water. She particularly enjoyed having her mother all to herself and even objected when I tried to go out with them one day. In a household of four children, Sonam Garjud had to fight for her place and for her mother's attention. The third child, Kabzung Tsomo, was Panjur's clear favorite, just as Tsetruk Dorje was Daka's. She was a charming little girl, and particularly adorable with her squint eye.

Padka had none of a parent's rose-tinted perspective on this. She asked me pointedly, "Who do the children look like?"

I replied, "Well, Tsetruk Dorje looks a lot like Aku Kungo, and the little baby girl also looks like them." I added, "Sonam Garjud looks like 'a little Padka.'"

She laughed happily and then asked with a cheeky look, "What about Kabzung Tsomo? What do you think?"

Embarrassed, I didn't answer.

Padka said, with a smile that made her eyes disappear, "Does she look like Ani Bamu? Does she, Achi Nyima? Hahaha!" She was referring mischievously to Tsering Panjur's mother, who was a lovely and well-liked person of slightly unfortunate looks.

"Oh, I don't know." I shook my head with embarrassment.

Padka chuckled at my discomfort and turned to kiss Kabzung Tsomo on her nose and mouth. "Oh, you look like Ani Bamu, don't you? Oh, you look like your grandmother, don't you?" she said to the smiling little girl. Then, turning to me again, she said slightly ruefully, "Her looks aren't very good, are they?"

Padka had a soft spot for the baby girl. She told me it was because she always loved children, particularly at that age, when they were small and quiet and didn't cause any trouble. I wondered if it was also because the little one looked like her first baby, the one who had passed away seven years ago. Whenever Padka came back to the tent from a day outside, she would always go first to the little girl and shower her with kisses and affection. The little girl was still feeding primarily on breast milk. She had not been planned but was clearly loved.

Early on, Padka had said to me, "This one has a salary. I mean, this one cost a salary."

I looked at her, puzzled, and so she explained more clearly. "We are allowed only three children, us Tibetan nomads. So when this one came, we had to pay a fine."

"How much did you have to pay?" I asked.

Padka hesitated and then said quietly, "Ten thousand."

My eyes widened, and she nodded in agreement.

"Really?!"

"Yes," she replied, nodding her head again. "It was almost all our caterpillar fungus money for the year."

Then turning to the baby girl, she smiled and said, "You have a salary, don't you, little one? A very big salary!"

"Wah," I said, digesting what she had told me. "Couldn't you have said it was Daka's baby?"

Padka looked at me and shook her head. She said gently, "But that's not good. Daka is not married, so if she had a baby, then they would fine her. That is not good, Achi Nyima. We just paid the fine."

"Yes, I see," I replied, rightly chastened.

The baby girl let out a little cry. Kabzung Tsomo had pinched her, trying to take away the flower that Padka had given her. There was a shout and then a loud smack. The tent filled with the sounds of Kabzung Tsomo crying very loudly and the little girl crying in sympathy.

Padka shook her head and said, "Having children hurts your ears, doesn't it, Achi Nyima? Stop crying, you two, you're hurting our ears!" She comically held her ears and feigned an expression of pain, but it didn't work this time. The crying continued.

On my last morning at Gatsong, we were again in the black tent in Shehoma, the autumn pasture. I said that I would leave after the morning milking was finished and the second meal was done. I had left in the past, but not since my first time living with them had I spent such a long time in their company. Moreover, this time I had arrived as a familiar. It had been a wonderful experience.

Over the meal, Padka asked, "Achi Nyima, when will you come back?"

I looked at her and replied truthfully, "I don't know. I think it will be another few years until I can."

She looked away quickly and then said to Daka, "I want to walk to Taraka."

Daka shook her head and said, "No, *I'm* going to walk with her to Taraka."

For the first time that I ever observed, the sisters looked like they were going to have an argument.

"But you went with her to Zaka yesterday," Padka said, almost petulantly. "I stayed here and looked after the milk. Let me go."

Daka remained firm. "No, *I'm* going to walk with her. I have to go to father's to pack the *chiwa* [dried yak dung] and leaves. You know that."

Padka stayed silent but hit Daka lightly with a dried branch from a *sera* shrub. When she caught my eye, she laughed half-heartedly. I felt strangely glad that they were arguing over who got to walk with me and then really sorry to leave. I didn't know when I would return.

When we had finished the meal, I got up to gather my things. I said a quick and simple good-bye to Padka, whose face had turned a little red and whose eyes had started to tear up. I touched my forehead to hers, feeling teary myself. Kabzung Tsomo and the baby girl looked on silently.

"Be well, Achi Nyima! Come back soon! Be well! Go slowly!" Padka called out as we walked toward the valley.

"Be well, Padka!" I cried back.

I stayed in the house for a while longer, talking with Aku Kungo, Daka, and Tsetruk Dorje before taking my leave. Touching my forehead to each of theirs, I promised to return. I had told Aku Kungo that we could com-

FIGURE 6.3
With Padka and her children, Shehoma, 2013. Photo by author.

municate through Tashi and that I would send news when I could. He looked at me with kindness and told me to come back soon. Daka walked me part of the way to Taraka. She did not say anything as we walked but held my hands tightly as we parted ways.

Glossary

achi (W: a ce) older sister

api (W: a ph'i) fresh cheese made from
   dara

'bu   *see* yartsa gunbu

chiwa (W: lci wa) dried yak dung used
   for fuel

chorten (W: mchod rten) Tibetan stupa,
   reliquary

chuba (W: phyu pa) long Tibetan robe

chura (W: phyur ra) dried cheese made
   from *dara*

dara (W: da ra) milk from which the
   cream/butter has been removed

dri (W: 'bri) female yak

drogmo (W: 'brog mo) female nomadic
   pastoralist

drogpa (W: 'brog pa) male nomadic
   pastoralist

droma (W: gro ma) edible tuber

dursa (W: dur sa) sky burial site

dzomo (W: mdzo mo) female hybrid
   cow-yak

fema (W: sped ma) kind of potentilla

genla (W: dge rgan) abbreviated version
   of *dge rgan lags*, respected teacher

gepa (W: skud pa) yarn or rope made
   from *tsi*

go re (W: go re) fried braids of wheat
   dough

gur (W: gur) summer tent made of white
   canvas

gya (W: rgya) Chinese person

gyamo (W: rgya mo) Chinese woman

hua ren (C) overseas Chinese person

ja ma bod (W: rgya ma bod) neither
Chinese nor Tibetan
jig ten (W: 'jig rten pa' lha) gods or
spirits of this world
jin (C) Chinese unit of measure;
approximately 600 grams
jin bur (W: dkyil 'bur/dkyus 'bur) small
head of a hill

ka kha ga nga (W: ka kha ga nga) first
four letters of Tibetan alphabet
karyang (W: kar yang 'bog tho) a kind of
rhubarb
katsa (W: kha tsha) animal illness; foot-
and-mouth disease
katsa metog (W: kha tsha me tog) species
of buttercup (*Ranunculus japonicas*)
khaliy (W: dka' las) term of greeting;
from dka', meaning "hard" or
"difficult"
khata (W: kha btags) ceremonial scarf,
usually white
khenpo (W: mkhan po) head lama
kora (W: skor ra) circumambulation
kulu (W: khu lu) soft down from the
undercoat of yaks
kyera (W: ske rags) tie, or belt, for a
Tibetan robe

lama (W: bla ma) generally translated
as "highest," "teacher"; indicates one
who is qualified to conduct rituals
langma (W: glang ma) species of willow
(*Salix thamsoni*)

latse (W: lha rtse) sacred cairns with
prayer flags
lawa (W: gla ba) Tibetan deer
lha yag (W: lha g.yag) god-yak; a yak
that has been liberated and offered to
a deity
losar (W: lo sar) Tibetan new year

magpa (W: mag pa) called-in son-in-law
maluh (vernacular) vernacular term of
endearment; usually reserved for
children and those younger than
oneself
mani prayer stones (W: ma ni rdo)
stones on which the chant "o mane
padme hum" has been carved
mi rab den (W: mi rabs bdun) seven
generations
mirtagpa (W: mi rtag pa) impermanence
misha (W: mi sha) blood feud; enemy
mo (W: mo) divination
modam (W: mo dam) fortune-teller;
diviner
momo (W: mo mo) steamed flour
dumplings

nei (W: nas) roasted barley flour
nyerma (W: snyag ma) a tall shrub with
purplish-red-tinged leaves that grows
in thick clusters
nyingma (W: rnying ma) old teachings; a
sect of Tibetan Buddhism

ra ma lug (W: ra ma lug) neither goat nor
sheep
rinpoche (W: rin po che) precious one

rtagpa (W: rtagpa) permanent phenomenon that always abides

sang (W: bsangs) smoke-purification ritual

sera (W: sur ra) species of rhododendron (*Rhododendron nivale Hook*)

shanyi (W: sha nye'i) cousin, relative

sha shinpa (W: bya sbyin pa) person responsible for cutting up a corpse for the sky burial

shedra (W: bshad grwa) Buddhist teaching college

shera (W: byu ru) coral

shizhuan (C) vocational college

shugpa (W: shug pa) species of juniper (*Juniperus formosana*)

siter giter (vernacular) dwarf hardy gloxinia (*Incarvillea compacta*) flower

tagma (W: stag ma) species of rhododendron (*Rhododendron przewalskii*)

tashi delek (W: skhra shi bde leg) Tibetan phrase expressing wishes of well-being and good fortune

terma (W: gter ma) treasure

terton (W: gter ston) treasure revealer

thangka (W: thang ka) traditional Tibetan cloth painting

thang shing (W: thang shing) fir tree

trim (W: khrims) decree

tsampa (W: rtsam pa) dish made of Tibetan roasted barley flour mixed with milk tea and butter

tshe thar (W: tshe thar) act of "liberating life"

tsi (W: rtsid) yak hair, cut from the tail and sides

Tuimu Huancao (C) Retiring Livestock, Restoring Pasture campaign

we'u (W: we'u) one-year-old yak calf

wo ae wog (vernacular) three-syllable imitative grunting sound used by Dora Karmo women to call their *dri*

worda (W: 'ur rdo) yak-hair slingshot

xiang zhengfu (C) township government

Xibu Dakaifa (C) Develop the West campaign

yartsa gunbu (W: dbyar rtswa dgun 'bu) caterpillar fungus (*Ophiocordyceps sinensis*)

zhi dag (W: zhing bdag, gzhi bdag) territorial deity

zhi mo chung chung (vernacular) little one [girl]

zho (W: zho) full-fat yogurt

zhorshi (W: zho shig) full-fat soft cheese, typical to this area of Minyag

zi (W: gzi) a kind of precious stone

Suggested Reading

Innumerable writers have deeply influenced my thinking, learning, and knowledge not only of anthropology and the ethnographic endeavor but also of the wider Himalayan region and the nomadic pastoralists who live on the Tibetan plateau. The following list—which is not intended to be representative—includes works that have been the most significant.

THE GENERAL ENDEAVOR OF ANTHROPOLOGY

Jackson, Michael D. 2010. "Where Thought Belongs: An Anthropological Critique of the Project of Philosophy." *Anthropological Theory* 9 (3): 235–51.

Kapferer, Bruce. 2013. "How Anthropologists Think: Configurations of the Exotic." *Journal of the Royal Anthropological Institute* 19: 813–36.

ETHNOGRAPHIC MEMOIRS

Craig, Sienna. 2008. *Horses Like Lightning: A Story of Passage through the Himalayas.* Boston: Wisdom Publications.

Jackson, Michael D. 1995. *At Home in the World.* Durham, NC: Duke University Press.

McHugh, Ernestine. 2001. *Love and Honor in the Himalayas: Coming to Know Another Culture.* Philadelphia: University of Pennsylvania Press.

Sam, Canyon. 2012. *Sky Train: Tibetan Women on the Edge of History.* Seattle: University of Washington Press.

TIBETAN COSMOLOGY AND RELIGION

David-Neel, Alexandra, and Lama Yongden. 1978. *The Superhuman Life of Gesar of Ling.* Berkeley, CA: Shambhala Publications.

Dorje, Gyurmed. 2005. *The Tibetan Book of the Dead: First Complete Translation.* New York: Penguin Classics.

Germano, David. 1998. "Re-membering the Dismembered Body of Tibet: Contemporary Tibetan Visionary Movements in the People's Republic of China." In Melvyn C. Goldstein and Matthew T. Kapstein, eds. 1998. *Buddhism in Contemporary Tibet: Religious Revival and Cultural Identity.* Berkeley: University of California Press.

Karmay, Samten G., ed. 1998. *The Arrow and the Spindle: Studies in History, Myths, Rituals and Beliefs in Tibet.* Kathmandu: Mandala Book Point.

Lhalungpa, Lama, trans. 1985. *The Life of Milarepa.* Boston: Shambala.

Samuel, Geoffrey. 1995. *Civilised Shamans: Buddhism in Tibetan Societies.* Washington, DC: Smithsonian Press.

Tan, Gillian G. 2010. "A Modern Portrait of a Tibetan Incarnate Lama." In David Templeman, ed. 2010. *New Views of Tibetan Culture.* Caulfield, Victoria, Australia: Monash University Press.

Tucci, Giuseppe. 1980. *The Religions of Tibet.* London: Routledge & Kegan Paul.

NOMADIC PASTORALISM IN EASTERN TIBET

Ekvall, Robert. (1968) 1983. *Fields on the Hoof: Nexus of Tibetan Nomadic Pastoralism.* Prospect Heights, IL: Waveland Press.

Norbu Rinpoche, Namkhai. (1959) 1997. *Journey among the Tibetan Nomads: An Account of a Remote Civilisation.* Dharamsala: Library of Tibetan Works and Archives.

Thargyal, Rinzin. 2007. *Nomads of Eastern Tibet: Social Organization and Economy of a Pastoral Estate in the Kingdom of Dege.* Leiden: Brill.

COMMUNITIES IN THE GREATER HIMALAYAN REGION

Adams, Vincanne. 1996. *Tigers of the Snows and Other Virtual Sherpas: An Ethnography of Himalayan Encounters.* Princeton: Princeton University Press.

Levine, Nancy E. 1988. *The Dynamics of Polyandry: Kinship, Domesticity, and Population on the Tibetan Border.* Los Angeles: University of California Press.

Mumford, Stan. 1989. *Himalayan Dialogue: Tibetan Lamas and Gurung Shamans in Nepal.* Madison: University of Wisconsin Press.

Ramble, Charles. 2008. *The Navel of the Demoness: Tibetan Buddhism and Civil Religion in Highland Nepal.* Oxford: Oxford University Press.

HISTORICAL CHANGES AND CONTEMPORARY VIEWS ON TIBET

Bass, Catriona. 1998. *Education in Tibet: Policy and Practice since 1950.* London: Zed Books.

Epstein, Lawrence, ed. 2002. *Khams pa Histories: Visions of People, Place and Authority.* Leiden: Brill.

Kolås, Åshild, and Monika Thowsen. 2005. *On the Margins of Tibet: Cultural Survival on the Sino-Tibetan Frontier.* Seattle: University of Washington Press.

Makley, Charlene. 2007. *The Violence of Liberation: Gender and Tibetan Buddhist Revival in Post-Mao China.* Berkeley: University of California Press.

McGranahan, Carole. 2010. *Arrested Histories: Tibet, the CIA and Memories of a Forgotten War.* Durham, NC: Duke University Press.

Ortner, Sherry. 1989. *High Religion: A Cultural and Political History of Sherpa Buddhism.* Princeton: Princeton University Press.

Shakya, Tsering. 1999. *The Dragon in the Land of Snows.* New York: Columbia University Press.

Yeh, Emily. 2013. *Taming Tibet: Landscape Transformation and the Gift of Chinese Development.* Ithaca, NY: Cornell University Press.

NOMADIC RESETTLEMENT

Bauer, Kenneth, and Huatse Gyal. 2015. "Introduction." *Nomadic Peoples* 19 (2): 157–63.

Foggin, J. Marc. 2008. "Depopulating the Tibetan Grasslands: National Policies and Perspectives for the Future of Tibetan Herders in Qinghai Province, China." *Mountain Research and Development* 28 (1): 26–31.

Gruschke, Andreas. 2012. "Tibetan Pastoralists in Transition: Political Change and State Interventions in Nomad Societies." In Hermann Kreutzmann, ed. 2012. *Pastoral Practices in High Asia: Agency of "Development" Effected by Modernisation, Resettlement and Transformation.* Dordrecht and New York: Springer.

Ptackova, Jarmila. 2011. "Sedentarization of Tibetan Nomads in China: Implementation of the Nomadic Settlement Project in the Tibetan Amdo Area; Qinghai and Sichuan Provinces." *Pastoralism: Research, Policy and Practice* 1: 4.

CATERPILLAR FUNGUS

Boesi, Alessandro, and Francesca Cardi. 2009. "Cordyceps Sinensis Medicinal Fungus: Traditional Use among Tibetan People, Harvesting Techniques and Modern Uses." *HerbalGram—The Journal of the American Botanical Council* 83: 52–61.

Sulek, Emilia. 2010. "Disappearing Sheep: The Unexpected Consequences of the Emergence of the Caterpillar Fungus Economy in Golok, Qinghai, China." *Himalaya* 30: 9–22.

Winkler, Daniel. 2009. "Caterpillar Fungus (*Ophiocordyceps sinensis*) Production and Sustainability on the Tibetan Plateau and in the Himalayas." *Asian Medicine* 5 (2): 291–316.

Yeh, Emily T., and Kunga Lama. 2013. "Following the Caterpillar Fungus: Nature, Commodity Chains and the Place of Tibet in China's Uneven Geographies." *Social and Cultural Geography* 14 (3): 318–40.

OTHER TEXTS MENTIONED IN THIS BOOK

Cohen, Brad. 2014. "The Haunting Sichuan-Tibet Highway." *BBC Travel*, May 20. www .bbc.com/travel/feature/20140417-the-haunting-sichuan-tibet-highway.

Hastrup, Kirsten. 1990. "The Ethnographic Present: A Reinvention." *Cultural Anthropology* 5 (1): 45–61.

Lindholm, Charles. 2003. "Culture, Charisma and Consciousness: The Case of the Rajneeshee." *Ethos* 30 (4): 357–75.

Sogyal Rinpoche. 1992. *The Tibetan Book of Living and Dying.* San Francisco: Harper Collins.

Tsing, Anna L. 2013. "Sorting Out Commodities: How Capitalist Value Is Made through Gifts." *Hau: Journal of Ethnographic Theory* 3 (1): 21–43.

Urry, John. 2002. *The Tourist Gaze.* London: Sage Publications.

Index

CPSIA information can be obtained
at www.ICGtesting.com
Printed in the USA
BVHW030503241218
536044BV00004B/10/P